tracking desire

For Marsey, with gratitude for your art in my life —

tracking desire

A Journey after Swallow-tailed Kites

SUSAN CERULEAN

Susan Cerulean

The University of Georgia Press
Athens and London

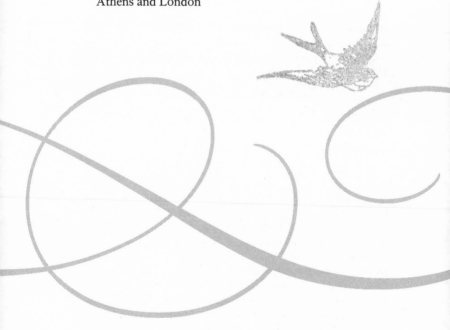

Designed by Sandra Strother Hudson
Set in Fournier
Printed and bound by Maple-Vail
The recycled, neutral pH paper in this book meets the guidelines
for permanence and durability of the Committee on Production
Guidelines for Book Longevity of the Council on Library Resources.
Printed in the United States of America
09 08 07 06 05 C 5 4 3 2 1

Library of Congress Cataloging-in-Publication Data
Cerulean, Susan.
Tracking desire : a journey after swallow-tailed kites / Susan Cerulean.
    p. cm.
Includes bibliographical references.
ISBN 0-8203-2697-6 (hardcover : alk. paper)
1. American swallow-tailed kite. 2. Nature—Psychological aspects.
I. Title.
QL696.F32C46 2005
598.9'45—dc22
2004024703

British Library Cataloging-in-Publication Data available

Earlier versions of portions of this work first appeared in the
following publications. Portions of "The Wild Heart of Florida"
and "Restorying Florida" in *The Wild Heart of Florida: Florida
Writers on Florida's Wildlands*, ed. Jeff Ripple and Susan Cerulean,
1–4 and 82–85 (University Press of Florida, 1999). Reprinted with
permission of the University Press of Florida. "Legend of the
Swallow-tailed Kite" in *Stories from Where We Live: The South
Atlantic Coast and Piedmont*, ed. Sara St. Antoine (Milkweed
Editions, 2004). "Searching for Swallowtails" in *The Woods
Stretched for Miles: New Nature Writing from the South*, ed. John
Lane and Gerald Thurmond (University of Georgia Press, 1999).
"Origin Moment" and "Writing the Birds" in *Elemental South: An
Anthology of Southern Nature Writing*, ed. Dorinda Dallmeyer
(University of Georgia Press, 2004). "Looking after God's Birds"
in *Intimate Nature: The Bond between Women and Animals*, ed.
Linda Hogan, Deena Metzger, and Brenda Peterson (Fawcett
Columbine, 1998).

This book is for David
and all the children,
especially those waiting to be born.
May they never have to choose
between science and spirit
or between their own hungers
and the survival of our only Earth.

The natural property of a wing is to raise that which is heavy and carry it aloft to the region where the gods dwell.

PLATO, *Phaedrus*

Contents

tracking desire

Origin Moment

It was over South Carolina's Edisto River that I saw my first swallow-tailed kite. My memory is etched with a clear image of how that bird swung into view and hung over me, suspended like an angel, so starkly black and white, with its wide-scissored split of a tail. I rushed to grab binoculars, almost flipped the canoe. The bird rode a breeze too subtle to sense, its breast a center point for the sleek maneuver of wing and tail, as if a kite string actually were attached to the deeply muscled breastbone. As suddenly as it appeared, the bird was gone.

Perhaps you have seen these wonderfully adroit flyers, living origami, drifting over a wild southern river, using their deep-forked tails as sensitive rudders. Although kites are large—with a wingspread wider than that of a red-tailed hawk—they are hard to keep in sight or follow very far. If you have been lucky enough to spot one, you probably hope to repeat the experience.

When that first fleet kite shadow darkened my face and I lifted my eyes, astonished, to watch the bird wheel above the river's sunny run, I knew that something essential connecting me viscerally to wildness had come into my life. I wanted that wildness. I wanted to leap out of the boat, to scramble over the abrupt knees of the cypress and climb the insufficient wild aster vines. I wanted to follow that bird.

Only now do I begin to have words for what I felt, half crouched within the confines of the silver canoe. I begin to name the wild desire that strained my body toward that awesome bird. I can begin to sketch how, in that swamp, my life fully opened to the world of the swallow-tailed kite, an unimagined gift from some god.

To me, kites are about surprise. Mystery. Being gifted. Except when they nest or gather to migrate, it is hard to specifically "bird" for swallow-tails. You can increase your chances of finding them by looking in the right places. It's best to just be in the right places and let them come to you. In this part of the world that means getting out on the rivers in the summer months. When I drive up the west coast of Florida, north from Tampa to my home in Tallahassee, climbing the ladder of latitude, I slow at each river crossing and look skyward: Little Waccasassa, Waccasassa, the broad Suwannee, the Steinhatchee, Spring Warrior Creek, the injured Fenholloway, the Econfina, the mysterious Aucilla, the Wacissa, the St. Marks, and dozens of creeks in between. I still can't be sure of seeing a kite, but that's how I increase my chances.

The swallow-tailed kite is a flexible and enterprising bird and, like life itself, intends to inhabit every place it can. A sky-rider, this raptor seems to affect the wetlands and the forests even less than most of the other birds do. The emerald marshes never feel the kite's full weight; nor do the great river-swamp forests. The bird will cleave the surfaces of our rivers and springs on the wing, to drink or cool its belly, splintering the calm for only seconds. When they are here, kites nest high in pines, picking thousands of dragonflies, wasps' nests, anoles, and small snakes from the foliage of the nearby forested wetlands, but neatly with their feet, never stopping their flight. For long stretches of time, as they raise a chick or two, kites go unremarked by human eyes.

Not so long ago, the swallow-tailed kite was able to build its nests as far into the continent's heartland as Minnesota; south and west to Texas; and then northeast to Maine. You might even have seen one in northern New Jersey in a good year—if you had been born before the turn of the twentieth century. Like many creatures, swallow-tailed kites have interacted little with humans, except to respond to human uses of the land. This particular bird's response has been an alarming decline in breeding range and population. Biologists like to draw

range maps of the creatures they study, indicating with color
bars and dashed lines where the animals nest, migrate, and overwinter. If you compare a present-day range map for the swallow-tailed kite with a presettlement range map for the bird (that
is, before the northern European colonizers brought this continent to its knees), the contemporary version looks as if someone had applied heat to a thin film of colored ink, shrinking it
into something so small that you want to cup your hand over the
page to protect from the frightful, drying air those bits of places
where kites still live.

I have never lived outside the kite's dwindled North American home range since I came to Florida thirty-four years ago. At
first, of course, I had no idea that I shared kites' diminished
space or even that they existed; but maybe, just as we are unconsciously formed by the living spirit of a landscape, we can be
drawn to our place and our work, even to something as specific
as the breeding range of a bird.

Among the Dagara tribe of West Africa, it is believed
that unborn children, approaching the end of their time in the
fastness of their mothers' wombs, know their purpose in the
world. In a ritual conducted during the mother's pregnancy, a
shaman-priest asks the child-who-is-to-come, "Tell us why you
have been sent, your purpose for visiting us." Through the
voice of his or her mother, who is in a trance, the child replies
to the shaman and other family members. The grandfather of
the child names him or her accordingly and later acts as con-
fidant and guide, helping the young one assume the life course
she or he indicated while still in utero.

Among my people, the northern Europeans translocated to
the North American continent during the past two hundred
years, I have imagined that another way used to be given to the
growing child to help her know her path: the tending of her
own origin moment.

For us, our human origin moment is the instant when our

base-rock, permanent images and assumptions begin to form as the planet becomes aware of itself through this new being, as it never has before. Wherever a child is located, all that she remembers, is her origin moment, and she will live her life forward from this moment of convergence, with whatever emotional overtones and cultural assumptions are included. Among my people, this occasion customarily happens between the ages of one and two years. In other times, the origin moment probably could be traced back much earlier, but our lives have constricted in matters of the old spirit ways.

These origin moments set the course of the lives of the wild animals, as well as the course of our own lives, and it is not so difficult to understand how the wind in the thin tops of tall pine trees informs even the embryos of swallow-tailed kite chicks in the egg and why kites forever return to such fragile circumstances to build their own nests as adults.

In my earliest memory, I stood alone in a crib, my hands gripping a smooth wooden rail, in a warm and darkened house. Outside a window, miles down and away to the southeast, blazed the brilliant electric lights of New York City. Between me and Manhattan Island, where my father went to work each day, I sensed the dark marshlands, the second-growth foothill forests, and the dimmed stars. I fell into my human awareness from this place of watching. Behind me, although I was just barely over a year old, slept my baby sister in a second crib. Beyond her bed was the closed door to my parents' bedroom. At the time memory and spirit recognized each other in the small child of my body, in the early 1950s in northern New Jersey, no swallow-tailed kites were anywhere nearby. It must have been January when I stood in my crib looking to the south and east, and it was dark outside, and kites do not often fly after dark nor in the winter cold. What I knew instead was the frosty outbreath of northern Appalachian trees, the fragrance they exhaled, and the way the snow melts on the south side of those trees and how cold shadows protect the snow on the northern exposure, striping the hillside white longer into spring than seemed bearable, especially for a (once again) pregnant mother of two very young children, such as my own mother. I knew that early winter darkness and the long spaces of the minutes between the drop of the dark and the hour when my father's train would return him home from New York City. Without even a word, my mother taught me this about time, how it is elastic, like the potential range map of a bird, and how it can drown you or bring you quickly to your heart's dearest dreaming.

So I would not have seen the swallow-tailed kite in my earliest years. The spring delivered robins in May (not the winter redbreasts that flock to the native hollies where I live now in north Florida), but never a kite. Until I was in my early twenties, my experiences of birds were surprised sorts of encounters, chancy moments, unpatterned. In kindergarten, I was taught songs about orioles and robins singing sweetly in spring, but no one knew or could convey the seriousness, or the dependability, or the pattern of their return. My family lived season to season, loving the natural world but not fully aware that we were actually of it. We thought of the birds, the seasons, the landscape, all things wild only as they affected our needs and comforts.

How was it, then, that I came to so love this wild bird and care for its continuance on our planet?

"I've got a new book to read to you children tonight," my father announced one evening in the winter of my seventh year. "It's about birds. And there's a special part for each of you to do, to help me tell the story. One of you each night." He settled himself comfortably against the headboard of the double bed he shared with my mother. Our family had grown to four children: girl (me), girl, boy, girl.

"Me first, me first," we all hollered, pushing in close, scrapping for his attention and the novelty of the new book.

"Oldest to youngest, this will be Susie's night," my father

said firmly. Happily surprised, I scrambled onto his lap, curling my toes into the white chenille bedspread. I crooked an arm around the channel of his neck, feeling privileged, singled out. Usually, the younger two went first. My second sister, Bobbie, quickly claimed our father's left side; the little ones staked out the foot of the bed. Dad tilted the big book so everyone could see, at least sort of, but I got to hold one endleaf of the new treasure myself. Dad opened *Birds of America* to the first page and began to read aloud an account of a single wild bird, the scarlet tanager. He told about where it lived, the colors of its feathers, how it constructed its nest, how many babies hatched from its nest. I listened, but all the time I was waiting for him to finish, because then I would be allowed to tear a picture sticker of that bird from a sheet of gummed postage-stamp images illustrating thirty-six of the kinds of birds appearing in the book. I could see that my youngest sister and brother wouldn't be allowed to do this part; they might rip across a stamp, which would ruin a bird, ruin the new ritual. They had begun to tussle on the end of the bed, their attention to the story already lost.

I stared at the image in my hand. Even though the sticker was flat and so much smaller than life size, the crimson of the bird's body entranced me, as did the ebony of its wings and tail.

"Lick the back of it," Dad said. "Stick it anywhere you want, on the scarlet tanager's page."

I touched my tongue to the back side of the stamp, activating the bitter glue, and pressed the picture firm against the page, as straight as I could manage. With my fingernails, I picked at the tiny ragged tears at the stamp's edge so my bird could float perfectly on the creamy white page of Dad's new book.

Perhaps my longing after birds was cemented on the summer deck of the *Miss Ocracoke,* one of the car ferries that transported people and their goods between Hatteras Island and Ocracoke to the south. As my mother steered our family station wagon aboard the ferry, I watched through the open window as laughing gulls and pelicans vied for perches atop the enormous harbor pilings. The ferry attendants moved between the cars, swinging heavy wooden blocks by short rope hanks, shoving them against the cars' front tires to hold them in place for the brief open-water crossing. Then we were allowed to scramble onto the flat gunmetal-gray deck. The air was rank with diesel fumes and the clank of chains. We felt the engine's growl through our feet. As the men cast off from the massive shoreside dock and hooked a chain across the ferry's stern, the seagulls lifted from the harbor pilings, collecting around us, dozens and dozens of them, each exactly alike, ebony-capped, screaming.

"Can we have some bread?" we begged our mother, but she waited until the boat entered the main channel, until the winds blew the diesel fumes out and away and the sharp salt air filled our lungs. Then she divided the bread she had brought into five portions—my share was one and a half slices of the squishy brown stuff (we never threw gulls the good bread, the white Pepperidge Farm sandwich loaf my father preferred). I tore at the crust, peeled it like the skin of an orange. It was too long to give away all at once, so I ripped it into chunks, pushing my wind-whipped hair from my eyes, as the birds circled and shrieked. Then I rolled torn fragments of the bread's interior into doughy balls; these had more weight on the wind and were easier to aim and toss.

Close, hungry, insistent, bold, brassy, the gulls approached like no other bird we knew. Their red feet dangled just over our heads, and their wings beat high. I tried to direct my bread toward a particular bird, maybe one a bit slower or more timid than the others. I liked to imagine that I was feeding an individual, that my offered food would matter to that bird, that we could be in relationship.

The ultimate achievement in feeding the ferry gulls was to lure one to feed directly from your hand. The birds didn't want to come this close; to take your bread in this way, they had to overcome an innate fear of humans. They had to give up their preferred method of feeding—the airborne snatch, with no contact. I slowed myself down into a deep patience, held back somehow, even though all around me, my siblings were yelling with delight and abandon, tossing their crumbs to the wind and the birds. I pushed away my own fear—that the bird would take some of my fingertip with the bread—and extended my arm straight out of its socket, long through the elbow, tried to will bread and hand and wrist into one, so that I could win the dare between us. Which of us wanted more fiercely: me, to feed the bird; or the gull, to eat my bread?

What I longed for was connection with a single bird, through my physical hand. I wanted to experience the particularity of my gift received and to believe that I could make a difference in the life of a single bird even. But the bird, once fed, would wheel away to gobble its prize, and I would lose sight of it in the general feeding frenzy at the ferry's wake.

Perhaps, like me, you have felt at your core some similar, perhaps unnameable longing, a hunger for intimacy (with a person or an animal or a landscape) that does not seem to correspond with the privileges and abundance of your life and that sometimes drives you to do or consume things you'd rather you hadn't. My journeys after kites have led me to understand that the power of our longings is placing the integrity of life on our tender emerald planet so greatly at risk. We stand, as Thomas Berry tells us, at the end of the Cenozoic era, the great flowering age of plant and animal diversity. Our own species must stare full face at the annihilation we are inflicting. I wonder about the fault lines in our own culture. What are the fractured places in our hearts and minds and spirits that have allowed us to stand by and watch, and even to participate in, the destruction of so much of life? How might we invoke transformative powers, very different from those that seem to rule our world just now?

The Roost

In the spring of 1993, I happened upon a flyer in the state wildlife library that brought me closer to kites than I ever could have imagined: the following Wednesday afternoon, the announcement read, Dr. Ken Meyer, a biologist with the National Park Service, would present a summary of his research on the status of swallow-tailed kites in south Florida. Seven days later, I sat before the man who knew more than I thought possible about a bird that had defined mystery for me for so long.

He wasn't a tall man, not macho nor self-promoting. But Ken Meyer's experimental designs were elegant, and he was posing big questions, on the brink of the kind of discoveries that come only to the committed. His hair was discreetly pony-tailed. He wore the requisite jeans and trim beard of the field biologist—the serious scientist's version, not like the graduate students who competed for "most ripped and hole-y clothes that will still stay on one's body."

Slide after slide flashed in the darkened room: images of kites up close, as I'd never seen them before. Pictures of their piney nesting places and of Ken's technicians holding one of the extraordinary creatures in hand, to measure and weigh. And then, incredibly, shot from the window of a small plane, a roost of one or two thousand kites resting high in the tops of trees, gathered together in midsummer, preparing to migrate to southern parts unknown. Over it all, Ken's voice, somehow already familiar, narrating in the dark, establishing what is known, and framing the next set of questions that he hoped to answer. With this scientist, I thought, excitement flaring butterflies in my belly, perhaps I could see kites when I wanted, not only by chance. At the end of the seminar, I introduced myself to Ken, struck up a conversation, told him I'd like to write a story about his research.

"Could I go out in the field with you sometime?" I asked. "Sometime soon?" He nodded yes.

A month later, in early August, it was arranged. My husband would transport our small son to school each morning, and a friend would retrieve him at day's end. For three days, I'd be free to follow kites. I drove six hours south to tiny LaBelle, in the heart of Florida's cattle country, about thirty miles and fifty years from the hustle and condos of Ft. Myers and Naples. I had no trouble renting a room in the LaBelle Motel; in high anticipation of the next morning's adventure, cut loose of the cadence of family and unable to sleep, I prowled the quiet back streets to the Caloosahatchee River. Live oak trees laden with Spanish moss, resurrection fern, and showy, pink-flowered bromeliads darkened the moon. It seemed a long, long waiting.

Eight o'clock the next morning, I located Ken Meyer at the deserted LaBelle airfield, screwing a radio antenna to the right wing of a Cessna 172.

"This is my pilot, Karen Dunne," he said, introducing a trim blonde woman cleaning the scratched plastic windows of her plane.

"Pleased to meet you," said Dunne. "Visibility is awful today—African-dusty. Got to have clear windows."

Minutes later the Cessna roared northeast. Quadrants of sugarcane fields, miles of them, unrolled beneath us. Heavily diked Lake Okeechobee glittered into view. Ken pointed out a deer picking a path through a stand of cabbage palms six hundred feet below. Fluffy doughnuts of cypress domes began to dot the landscape—I sensed the mood of Meyer and Dunne grow more serious as they scanned the horizon for kites.

"The birds are really sitting tight this morning," said Dunne through her headphones.

"They're still waiting for the air to rise," reassured Meyer. Except for the African haze, the sky was empty. No birds anywhere.

And then, all of sudden, directly below, a roost of nearly two thousand swallow-tailed kites hung like exotic black-and-white blossoms on a tight cluster of Australian pines. More kites than all but a handful of people will see in their lifetime. Our plane circled five times, allowing Ken to count and recount the birds, snap pictures, listen for radio signals. I watched the plane's tiny shadow caress the still mass of resting birds, flitting over their white heads weightless as a dragonfly. The birds didn't budge.

In the Cessna's back seat, I was less impressed with the spectacle of the birds than with their circumstances. Here was almost half of the world's population of this kite species, perching on brittle exotic trees on an earthen dike in the middle of highly altered Big Sugar terrain. Now that's vulnerable.

After the fifty-three-minute flight, we drove to breakfast at Flora and Ella's, a popular country restaurant just west of LaBelle. As we waited for eggs and biscuits, I spread a Florida atlas on the table, hungry for Ken to tell me more.

"Here is the historical heart of swallow-tailed kite breeding in Florida," Ken said, after a long swallow of coffee. On my map, he traced a broad backward S curve that ran from Miami north and west, around Lake Okeechobee, then skated east and north between Lakes Okeechobee and Istokpoga, straight north up the Kissimmee Prairie, and finally a gentle reverse curve north and west along Lakes Kissimmee and Tohopekaliga. He tapped a forefinger on the location of the staging roost we'd just flown over.

"And I'm surmising that's why the roost is located, maybe even must be located, right here, in the middle of this remaining arc of habitat," he said.

What I was growing to like about listening to Ken was how he always tried to frame what he knew in the largest possible context. What I didn't like was hearing the things that worried him. Because what concerned Meyer most about these birds, who very competently move between North and South America twice a year, was that remarkable gathering, the roost itself.

"As far as we know," he told me, "more than half of the

North American population of swallow-tailed kites funnels down through the peninsula of Florida every summer and briefly stops right here." He punctuated the urgency of his words again with a jabbing finger on my map. I carefully circled that exact spot with a faint pencil mark.

"Presumably, they're getting fat and waiting for favorable winds to migrate south," he said.

Meyer worried, first, that the roost was unprotected. The land where the birds gathered was owned by an indifferent, powerful corporation not known for its gentle handling of indigenous species. Second, the vast and diverse landscapes where the birds nested and foraged were under enormous siege from agricultural development.

"And third," said Meyer, "we have absolutely no idea where they are going when they leave south Florida. Or what human-induced threats they encounter once they reach their wintering grounds in Central or South America."

In the white glare of Flora and Ella's graveled parking lot, before we parted ways, Ken promised that I could accompany him to see the kites nesting next spring. I so looked forward to the certainty of seeing kites and learning about their lives through the eyes and accrued knowledge of an expert.

As I drove north, toward home, I realized that going out in the field with Ken Meyer to see swallow-tailed kites revived a yearning I'd suppressed for years. Now I couldn't stop thinking about them and their threatened status. I could not bear to think of the world without them. Instead of being satisfied with the trip I'd just taken, I urgently wanted more. More time in the wild, apprenticing to the man who knew what kites were about. I wanted to learn for myself, in person, what kites needed, what their bottom line was. I had to know what the essentials of their life requirements might be. If we could only isolate those needs into discrete packages, I thought, as I had learned in college biology classes—what do they need to eat? What habitats do they require to nest, to migrate, to forage, to overwinter? How do we protect them from predators, and by the way, what are their predators? If these things were known, then it would just be a matter of management. Then we—the lovers of kites, of all that is rare and wild—could see to each of those requirements, ultimately keeping safe the species as a whole, no matter what else happened in Florida.

Looking for Love

"Swallow-tailed kites are so damn synchronous," lamented Ken Meyer as we laced on our boots in the parking lot of Big Cypress National Park headquarters in the southern tip of Florida. Spring had come round again, and Ken was searching for nests, as many as he could find, gathering essential data for a long-term population study. He hadn't forgotten his invitation for me to join him in the field for a day or two.

I took his anxiety as a cue to hurry my preparations, quickly smearing sunscreen over my face and arms. I sure didn't want to be the reason he didn't get his work done that day.

"Almost every nest I've found in the Big Cypress region was built between March 29 and March 30," the biologist said, firing up his truck, double-checking over his shoulder to make sure water bottles, maps, and binoculars were stowed in the compartment behind our seat. "That means the conspicuous, visible business of courtship and nest-building—the period of time I can actually locate kite nests—is extremely limited."

We headed twenty-five miles east to Eleven-Mile Road, driving through freshly green dwarf-cypress forest. The ancient trees were widely spaced, hundreds of years old, perhaps six to ten feet tall. The ground was sparsely grassed, rough with lime rock, and recently dry. South Florida was at the end of its annual dry season, a time when, traditionally, wading birds and many other species nest and rear their young.

As we bumped along the dusty road, I tried to imagine the incredible convergence of hundreds of pairs of swallow-tails in this part of the state, all of them building their nests and laying their eggs within several days of one another, at most. I recounted what a refuge manager had told me: "You can set your calendar by them. They are entirely reliable."

Ken told me more: "In a sense, the forces of natural selection have cut a deal with swallow-tailed kites, and the birds' end of the bargain has a lot to do with being on time. Kites are among the first of the neotropical migrants to arrive in North America to nest and rear their young. Pairs of kites whose nests fail, usually because eggs or chicks were blown down by high winds, do not attempt to re-nest like many species do."

Continuing north on the crunchy gravel road, we gradually entered pine-dominated uplands. Ken parked the truck. We were looking for stands of twisty, gnarled pines with flattened crowns because that is where kites like to nest. Fine black ash sifted into my boots as I walked. Fire, a critical part of the landscape's natural cycle, had recently run through these woods. Understory vegetation—wax myrtle, myrsine, saw palmetto—appeared thoroughly scorched, but I knew it was only a temporary remission. Ken instructed me to scan the tallest pine in each stand of trees, explaining why nests were most likely to be found there.

"Despite their aerial prowess, kites don't maneuver well at low air speeds," he said. "We suspect that's one reason why they build their nests in wind-exposed tree tops. Watch when an adult kite leaves the nest—it won't simply flap away."

As if on cue, a kite dove toward the ground, wings tucked close to its body in a free fall. I sucked in my breath as it hurtled toward the ground, extended its wings, caught the wind, and sailed upward in a long glide.

Before long, Ken spotted another kite in one of last year's trees. I couldn't believe that the tree's tiny crown could support a nest, and it took a lot of looking for me to pick out the nest through my binoculars. Ken pointed out the fresh bowl of lichen that indicated an active nest, just the merest clump of green, from where we stood sixty feet below. Even better, a female hunkered down on the nest. Overhead, her mate and a third bird circled and called.

Through the transparent plume of purplish smoke, thunderheads congealed. It started to mist. The birds were agitated by our presence, another good sign of active nesting. We backed off a distance acceptable to the birds and watched the two attendants swoop and soar.

"What are they doing?" I asked.

"Just being territorial," Ken replied, enjoying the sight as much as I. One came in with a wriggling lizard for the female's dining pleasure. In the same way that kites snatch nesting material on the wing, they forage in the forest canopy for arboreal frogs, lizards, nestling birds, and even small snakes to feed their young.

The third kite circled the nest, always watching, courting the female with conspicuous dangling prey, cajoling her with call notes. More often than not, the pair ran the "extra" bird off. "Who are these extra birds?" I asked.

"Maybe an unmated juvenile, trying to attract attention," joked Ken, imagining a kite "personals" ad. "Looking for a lasting relationship, likes quiet walks, nonsmoker, check out this lizard—I'm a good prospect!"

We resumed our search. It was hard to look for the kites while walking through the rocky pine woods. Thickened roots of saw palmetto, cypress knees, ankle-twisting solution holes, and loose chunks of lime rock formed a continuous booby trap, yet the work of finding kites depended on never looking down, always toward the sky. Ken told me that the writer Peter Matthiessen refers to swallow-tailed kites as "God's birds" in his novel *Killing Mr. Watson;* the logic is that only a heavenly overseer can view this high-flying bird's steely blue back, reflecting the sky.

At dusk we walked among some freshly burned pines to listen to the preserve's night sounds, strictly for our own pleasure. The kites had long gone to roost. Smoke from the controlled fires had settled down close to the ground, and the woods were all black and green and sunset. We listened to the monoto-

nously repetitive calling of the chuck-will's-widow, the hoot of
a barred owl, and watched the nearly full moon sail into view.

"I never thought I'd live in Florida," Ken told me as we
swapped stories about our New Jersey roots. "But it seems that
I've got this melancholy attraction to wild landscapes. For me,
it's like a crush, I have no control, it just kind of washes over
me when I'm out in places like this."

"I think I know what you mean," I said. "But tell me more
about your melancholy. And why did you rule Florida out when
you talk about where you might end up living?"

"Florida is too much like where we grew up," Ken said, re-
ferring to Asbury Park, the Jersey shore resort town where he
was born and where my own family often summered. "The little
vestigial wild places I loved as a child were always being destroyed, turned into subdivisions. I saw this happen over and
over again, and I understood it, even at the age of eight.

"I had this feeling—it's all going away, and I can't stop it. I
still feel that way. The very least I can do is to try not to participate in the diminishment of the wild things I love. I suppose
that's at the bottom of my work with kites and why I like working on public land like this preserve; I can let down a little on a
night like this and believe this will all still be here in twenty
years."

What we didn't say in the beautiful dark night, as we headed
back to our respective rooms in the field station, was how the
fate of the kite might hang on more than just the public lands
remaining. That would be going far beyond mere melancholy.

"I was fated, so I thought, to participate in the diminishment
of things I cherished, and that idea made me crazy," said the
writer William Kittredge of his own childhood in rural western
Oregon.

As a child growing up in suburban New Jersey, I was
given time enough to dream among the trees. With my sister

Bobbie, I crafted little worlds among the fissured roots of our backyard poplars, amassing and arranging stores of acorn cap bowls, sassafras berries, miniature moss beds, and the handled swords of tulip poplar fruits. We'd smash and grind the acorns into a damp salmon meal, rich and substantive but bitter to the tongue, foodstuff for fairies we never saw, while the true birds built lives and nests just over our heads. One of those birds fell into my world on a spring Saturday, at least one bird, for there is a family snapshot of me holding a fledgling oriole on my thumb and forefinger. I was about eight years old, grave faced, with braided pigtails and bangs clipped high on my forehead. The lemon-breasted bird sat erect, its wings and tail too stubby to allow for flight. I cannot remember if the nestling tumbled too early from its nest into my fairy commissary on the forest floor or if a cat brought it to our glass-paned dining room door. I have no memory at all of how it came to rest on my finger or where it went from there. But here it is, a picture.

Saturday mornings, our mother would order us out of the house. "It's way too pretty to stay indoors," she'd say. She'd pack a wagon with peanut butter sandwiches and lemonade and send us to play by the neighborhood creek.

So that even if we didn't know, weren't taught, the actual names of more than five or ten kinds of birds, they must have been all around us. Maybe a thrush, slipping through the shrubbery overhanging the rock dams we built in the creek. Surely owls called outside the open windows when we slept, and chickadees plucked tangles of hair we combed from our brushes on the brick patio behind our house. "Do that outside," my mother would say, and so we did, leaving behind tumbleweeds of our gold and brown hair. And the chickadees must have pulled the silky stuff from the bricks that had snagged it, wound those filaments into bowls that held their own young, cupping our lives in this way around the naked bodies of baby birds. We never knew it, but still they were there, the many kinds of birds native to the foothills of northern New Jersey, and the animal in our bodies must have registered their voices, even without teachers to point out a *dee-dee-dee* from a *ʒʒʒ-ʒeep!*

The next morning dawned still and warm. Before eight, Ken and I were back at Raccoon Point. We left the truck and followed a swamp buggy trail, which also served, the tracks and scats told us, as a raccoon superhighway. We noticed, too, the footprints of otter, deer, and bobcat, and Ken told me to keep a close watch for panther tracks, as well. The preserve's birds were much more active this morning. Pine and prairie warblers, great crested flycatchers, white-eyed vireos, an assortment of woodpeckers, loose strings of white ibis: each attended to the first business of the day in its own way.

I admired the black-and-golden-winged dragonflies plying the sawgrass. Ken said they hadn't yet hatched when he was here last week; nor were the tree frogs calling. The way he saw it, with such abundant prey now available, the freshly migrated kites could feed with abandon and quickly get up to breeding condition.

We were especially keeping an eye out for kites carrying food or nesting material. Ken located another old nest and then, quickly, close by, a new one. Four kites swung above us, clearly agitated by our presence. I asked why they might have picked that particular tree. Ken speculated that the dangling moss or a twig remaining in a high crotch of the tree might act as a "releaser" for them, stimulating or reminding them that they had successfully raised young here the previous year. The birds whistled and called repeatedly—high, clear, urgent—and circled about thirty feet above us. We flagged the tree with orange tape and quickly moved north, a four-kite escort directly overhead, twisting and watchful but gradually silent.

The breeze picked up, and Ken herded me back to the truck, ever mindful of the very narrow window of time he had to find the number of nests his study design required. Clouds generated by the warm, foggy morning massed up and sailed northwest to the gulf. Several dozen wood storks climbed aboard the same breeze and wheeled away. Soon it would be too windy for the kites to carry nesting material, and they would drift off to forage until late afternoon.

By that time, I'd be driving north, my head and heart full of all I'd seen, the miles I'd walked in that wild landscape, so new to me, with kites all around. Purposeful kites, intent on territory and nesting. A purposeful man, intent on the kites. And me, traveling to be with them all for some not completely clear purpose and now returning home.

Soon, I would slow on the long clay road at my journey's end, bumping slowly over and around familiar potholes, their depth dependent on how recently the county grader had come our way. I'd check for loggerhead shrikes on the wires and indigo buntings in the small clump of willows to the south. I would turn at the last black mailbox on the left before the road dead-ends. The metal gate to our drive would be open, as it always is. Since it drags the ground a bit, we rarely pull it closed. The mailbox lacks a red metal postal flag, but all the letters of our names are still intact. I would slow even further to enjoy the short, canopied approach to the house between the tall hickories and oaks, lime rock crunching under the tires of my car. There would be rough wild sunflowers burning in the sun, a tangle of weeds where the spring vegetables grow, and always a rose or two in bloom.

The clearing where I lived with my husband and our six-year-old son, David, wanted to take itself back. I knew this by the way it kept dropping the winged seeds of red maple, the nuts of hickory, and all manner of ground-loving weed plants into the open places we were trying to coax into pasture. What we wanted was sunshine and a place for Easter egg hunts. And we wanted vista, even though this was a land that longed to return itself to white oak and wax myrtle, tall pine and live oak, a hardwood stand segueing into streamside hammock on the property adjoining us to the east. We wanted to see what was coming our way.

To hold on to our blueberry bushes and flowerbeds and the perennials by the drive, we constantly had to delineate the woods' edges and the pasture. This we did by mowing; but the understory of the woods we held open with fire. Tonight, such fire is ringing through the back two acres of oak woods; we have set these flames, knowing this to be the natural way of the woods. We don't allow the fire to burn near the greatest oaks—we rake the ground bare at their gnarly bark feet; they can't abide the scorching. But we run it low over the rest of the ground, hoping to transform the chiggers and the briers into something more benign. We three stand in the dark, watching fire, eating baked sweet potatoes for our supper. Butter runs between our fingers; we balance the steaming pink meat of the potato from hand to mouth. David is pleased that I did not bring forks and plates from the house.

Now my son is singing, as my husband tends the fire with shovel and rake. *Fire, fire, we are calling. Fire, fire, we are calling. Come, come, be with us tonight.* The tiny flames lick all the growing and dead things in their low-to-the-ground path. I listen to the green water-oak leaves snapping like bacon in a cast-iron frying pan. They are filled with something dense and living. With that sound, they release into hot ash, curling into the night sky. I see myself holding like the sage-colored leaves, wanting this small island of living, pushing away changes I haven't exactly mapped out, seen the boundaries of, planned for.

In the morning, a spare ebony ash will carpet our woods; beyond it, in the faraway spring, will come unknown wildflowers—and kites.

On my next trip south, Ken told me: "Finding kites in Everglades National Park is ridiculously easy. In fact, I'm willing to predict exactly where we will see them courting and building their nests: in two long patches of remnant pineland,

Pine Island and Long Pine Key, the largest stands of this plant community remaining in Dade County."

Ken was monitoring nesting success among the small but persistent population of swallow-tails in the Everglades, all that remained of an extensive population that once flourished north along the pinelands of the Miami Rock Ridge and the Gold Coast. Over the past six years, he had found twenty-eight nests in that single bit of pine forest.

Approaching the park, we drove through miles of agricultural fields peppered with huge irrigation rigs. Pesticide drift clung to the damp morning air. Pickups piled with cucumbers and sweet corn hurtled north. At the perimeters of the squared-off vegetable fields crouched old school buses packed with farm laborers ready for the day's work. I didn't like to think that this was where my produce came from.

We pulled into the visitor center parking lot, quickly ticking off a short list of birds: meadowlark, bobwhite quail, blue jay, downy woodpecker, fish crow, prairie warbler. No kites. We waited, finishing our coffee, leaning on the hood of the truck.

At 7:45 a.m., still no swallowtails. I felt a little impatient, wondering how they could actually be there without our seeing them against the open sky, through the thin pines.

But sure enough, when the morning breeze finally rose and touched my face, a kite cruised directly over us, riding that first breath of the day. We hopped into the truck, followed the bird half a mile, turned left, parked. How much easier could it get? The kite planed low into the pines and—snap!—broke off a twig with his feet. I actually saw and heard this subtle fact of reproduction, and my body surged with excitement.

The bird shifted the twig to his beak, lost it, plunge-dived twenty feet to retrieve it in midair, and then secured it, firmly this time, in his beak.

We watched and listened as he contact-called his mate, and I spotted the nest—my first. Ken advised me to watch for copulations.

"Sex usually follows some transfer of goods," he explained. "It all comes down to commodities."

Not this time, though. The female worked the twig into her nest start, and the male set out for more. She stayed, white head gleaming against the green, riding her treetop in a sea of Everglades wind.

I followed Ken into the pine woods, struggling several hundred feet over solution holes and pinnacle rock, to flag the nest tree for later observation by Ken and his crew. I raised my arms overhead to pass through chest-high stands of poison ivy and tropical poisonwood shrubs.

The nest tree was an absurd spindle of a pine. I could encircle it with one arm, and I did. Its tuft of canopy was no bigger than one of Dr. Seuss's truffula trees in *The Lorax*. And just about as endangered. The pinelands of Everglades National Park are the only contiguous examples that remain of this once common plant community in Dade County. In a 1996 national study of endangered ecosystems, scientists determined that the entire south Florida landscape, including the Everglades and the pine rockland habitats we were visiting that day, was so seriously degraded that it was deemed the most endangered ecosystem in the whole United States. Dr. Reed Noss based his comparison on the decline in original area of the ecosystem since European settlement; the present area it occupies; and the imminence of threat to, and number of, species listed by the federal government as threatened and endangered.

It isn't just in Everglades National Park that the options for kites may be closing down. Throughout most of south Florida, native habitat is converted to human uses at a record-breaking pace. The squeeze on natural lands is compounded by the region's management of its most controversial commodity, its defining feature: water. Only one hundred years ago, the topography of the state from Orlando to Florida Bay was a finely tuned natural system inhabited only by wild creatures keyed to the annual cycle of floods and droughts.

Today, the "River of Grass," corralled into an area half its historical size, is expected to supply the water needs of more than three million people, as well as enormous farms of sugar-cane, vegetables, and citrus that produce $750 million in yearly sales.

In particularly wet years, the natural systems, including the Everglades Conservation Areas, the park itself, and Big Cypress National Preserve, unnaturally brim with floodwaters—they are tasked to keep dry the Gold Coast metropolises to the east and the farms to the north. Flood control officials and farms pump their excess water into the Everglades, so much so that its animal inhabitants either starve to death or drown. For example, last summer at least sixteen hundred deer roamed the Ever-glades Conservation Areas. Six months later, after one of the wettest years on record, biologists feared that up to 80 percent of that herd was dead, trapped on shrinking tree islands or levees with nothing left to eat and nowhere, absolutely nowhere, to go.

For swallow-tailed kites, Ken Meyer guessed this was an equally disastrous year in south Florida.

"Probably because of the high water all over south Florida, we've had a heck of a time finding nests. Over the past six years, the average amount of time just to find a single nest was fifteen hours; this year, the average time to simply find one nest was over thirty-three hours. Also, we've gotten a lot fewer observations from other people. Kites tend to be numerous and conspicuous in south Florida, and this year, they just are not."

"What makes the kites leave?" I asked. "They nest so high, it doesn't seem like the water level would affect them."

We discussed the theory of our mutual friend, biologist Paul Moler. The successful reproduction of the kite's primary prey species, including arboreal frogs, snakes, and lizards, is knocked back by unnatural flooding. For example, certain of the frogs are adapted to lay their eggs during the dry summer months, in temporary isolated wetlands where their predators are minimal and their tadpoles can grow safely to maturity. During high water, predacious fish and insects roam the evenly flooded terrain, devouring the tender tadpoles that might one day have fed fledgling kites. In short, there probably isn't enough to eat.

"So where are they? Where do they go in a year like this?" I asked.

"Well, I had a call from John Cely up in South Carolina. He has seen one of our tagged birds from several years back up his way. And a swallow-tail was recently admitted to a rehabilitation center in Charlotte, North Carolina, that was found shot up there. I'd say they are wandering north from here, looking for better opportunity."

To make matters worse, in 1992 Hurricane Andrew broke or uprooted at least a third of the area's pines, in most cases the largest ones—and the very best candidates for kite nesting. Several years later, the wind-stressed survivors still bowed to that deadly wind, and pine bark beetles were slowly killing many of them. As in Big Cypress, these southern slash pines are basically rooted in lime rock. We inspected the upended root ball of an Andrew casualty. Its withered grip clutched more whitened rock than soil. Where will the kites go when these nest trees are gone?

All the time we talked, we watched the swallow-tails dropping a twig in one tree, then another.

Ken pointed out: "Can you see how these birds are restless, less focused than the Big Cypress kites? I'm anxious about what they will use for nesting material, a critical factor in the successful rearing of young kites."

The Spanish moss and lichens kites typically fashion into a nest matrix had been basically scoured from these woods, swept away toward Texas on Andrew's fury, Ken said. Last breeding season, just months after the destructive hurricane, the combination of fewer pines to nest in and virtually no nesting material was hard on the kites. Ken found only two nests, and only one young bird fledged.

A month later, Keith Bildstein, director of Hawk Mountain Sanctuary in Pennsylvania, checked in with Ken. Three swallow-tailed kites had shown up in Berks County, establishing a new county record and exciting hundreds of birdwatchers from New York to Washington, D.C. Bildstein thought that the visiting birds were essentially reclaiming territory held by their species more than two hundred years ago.

When I called Bildstein myself, he told me: "I think the conditions down there in Florida, which normally supports most of the country's swallow-tailed kites, were so bad that the birds just dispersed, which is how they react to adverse nesting conditions. But though we now have fascinating evidence that these birds can and will disperse all over the Southeast and even as far north as Pennsylvania when nesting conditions are abysmal in Florida, their status is vulnerable."

"I don't believe they can recolonize those lost portions of their historical breeding range all that easily," said Ken. "They simply may not have the behavioral flexibility to relocate as a group to a new area."

He continued: "What we see the birds do down here around Miami is continuously try to disperse out into their former range around here—what were once the pinelands of the Miami rock ridge."

But most of these native pines are long gone, lost to urbanization, so the birds attempt nesting in what looks to them like the next best thing: Australian pines. These non-native, highly invasive trees look like nest sites equivalent to the vanished south Florida slash pines from the kite's airborne perspective, but they are flimsy, wind-tossed, and easily broken. Five out of six swallow-tail nests in Australian pines fail, spilling the year's fertility for that pair of kites to the ground. Since these birds are so persistent, so behaviorally inflexible, their range here in south Florida acts like a sink, a sort of LaBrea tar pit. They return from South America to nest, spot the visual cue that triggers a "nest here!" response, and do so. But that visual cue is false advertising. The Australian pines cannot structurally support the eggs through incubation, and a breeding season is lost.

As I watched the birds loft in the morning sky, I contemplated what seems like a case of misplaced loyalty on their part. There was something familiar about how insistently they were trying to nest in a place that supported reproduction for their species so well for aeons but does no longer.

How Did We Get Here?

Kites (including, in Florida, swallow-tailed, Mississippi, snail, and white-tailed) rank among the most efficient wind masters in the bird kingdom. Their wings are designed to allow nearly stationary gliding against the wind, a type of flight aptly named "kiting." A deeply cleft tail and very light wing loading assist in providing the bird with the remarkable maneuverability required to capture flying insects midair and small animals such as frogs and snakes from the treetops during flight.

Brian Millsap, a wildlife biologist with the Florida Game and Fresh Water Fish Commission, once told me about a time he watched kites rocketing down and through a violent summer storm in south Florida. "We watched the birds begin a thousand feet up in the sky and come shooting down through all that lightning and wind. They were clearly enjoying the superfast rides generated by the storm, as if it were a giant roller coaster," he said.

Hunting from the sky as they do, swallow-tailed kites are extremely visual creatures. Along with the hawks, their eyesight is among the most acute of all birds. I imagine looking down at the land from their perspective. What are the things they notice? Although the clouds are our primary landmarks in the Florida sky, kites probably respond to that sky and the wind mostly through intuition. I can almost feel, myself, the outer primary feathers extended like sensitive fingers, constantly adjusting to air currents, and that delicate edge of blending, where the motion of the electrons of the feather and those of the air merge into the thing called flight.

The silhouette of the kite is so unsubstantial high in the sky, especially when it flies with vultures. If I see two kites soaring with four black vultures, my eye is immediately drawn to the bulk of the heavy-bodied vultures. Within seconds, the kites have outclimbed the vultures in the thermal, as if they were on an independent elevator, their profiles contracting wafer-thin, unsubstantial, to a memory or a dream of a thing that once was here.

To a kite's eyes, a hundred critical cues are offered; as the birds flock together in large numbers, just before migration, their communal eyes and ears are tuned to locate and exploit any abundant food sources in the area. Around Moore Haven and Lake Okeechobee, in July and August, the kites concentrate on the flying insects that share their airspace—dragonflies, grasshoppers, many others—their prey. And always, on the mounting and swirling and gathering of others of their kind, a checking in and out of community, the reference point for food, for safe resting, for unity.

I often wonder what draws the kites back to our continent each spring and which are the visual cues that pull them north. Do they begin in the Keys and move up to us, following the wriggling line of the salt creeks and then the rough green tumble of the forested bottomlands along the great rivers? Do they drop exhausted into the first high pine or coast in with no beating of the wings, just an easy slide from the Yucatán, no effort?

And how does Florida look through their eyes? When I fly north from Miami or Orlando to Tallahassee in a small airplane, what I see is broken landscape, long blocks of clear-cut pine, stretches of citrus ever more mechanized, chains of golf course communities, and then house upon house upon house upon highway. We cannot mimic the high flight of the kites in any real sense, but we can profit, we Floridians, by imagining the kite's view, the long view, of this fragile peninsula, and taking very careful note.

From a rickety lawn chair on the forest floor, I watch swallow-tailed kites, two restless adolescent chicks with tawny, dark breasts and heads, hunkered in their high pine nest in central Florida's Highlands Hammock State Park. Movement, height, and wind, their birthright. I'm on my way south again, this time to Avon Park, where I'm looking forward to observing Ken and his team actually band baby kites in their nests. I've stopped here on my way down, camping for the night. Ken alerted to me to the presence of this nest when we spoke by phone several days ago.

The smaller bird crouches just inside the thick lip of the twiggy nest bowl, shifting its weight from foot to foot. Perched on a branch about two feet away, a second, heavier chick picks at the transmitter harness Ken's crew fitted to its body just yesterday. The feathers of both birds riffle and rise at odd angles in the light gusty breeze. The larger bird extends its wings fully, then teeters in the barest wind, testing the properties of the element that will soon support it the rest of its life.

As I watch, an adult kite passes quickly through the branches above the nest, calling *wheet, wheet, wheet, wheet, wheet, wheet.* The chicks' response is imperceptible. The smaller one scratches its head. The other twists to preen its back, seeming to unhinge its tail at a ninety-degree angle as it does so. Within days, these birds will master flight and not return to such a single-pointed existence until they sit on eggs of their own some years from now. They will mount the high thermals with hundreds of their kind, and the bright Florida sun will bleach the brown streaking feathers of their youth into pure white spirit.

Early this morning, I passed a solitary hiker, a sweet-faced man with styled, curly hair, a plaid shirt, a walking stick.

He spoke unexpectedly: "This place is so abundant. It's almost too much!"

And I flashed back to my first trip to Highlands Hammock, how overwhelmed I was by the exceptional girth of the virgin hardwoods and cypress, the throbbing green life of the place, subtitling the park in my own mind as "the wild heart of Florida."

I said to the stranger: "Yes, and all of Florida used to be like this." Not a very engaging response.

It's because of what is happening to my state. Even the parks and protected lands seem worn. On the tiresome, eight-hour drive from Tallahassee yesterday, I saw plenty of bleak new development—and not a single swallow-tailed kite. In fact, between Ocala and Lake Placid on U.S. 27, I got the clear impression that the whole state was for sale, and to anyone's specifications, and really cheap. New subdivisions and mobile home parks sprouted along the state's spine of ancient sand dunes, offering seductive promises such as "permanent home quality at mobile home prices." The entrances to these places resembled used car lots, or carnivals, strung with plastic red, white, and blue pennants that snapped and jumped in the breeze. The individual flags were imprinted with enticing messages:

"Sale! Rock bottom prices!"

"Golf, golf, golf!"

"Welcome!"

Larger billboards described the things for sale in more detail:

"Leisure Lakes Lifestyles Fore You!"

"Tropical Hardwood Estates: Manufactured Homes from the $30s"

"Polo Park: Lakefront Retirement Living"

Mile after mile, Florida, and living in Florida offered up as effortless, at the expense of whatever lived here before. And yet every one of us, a staggering nine hundred new residents each day, arrives eager to embrace our new place, even if we don't know what it really is or once looked like.

Just as I was when I first moved to St. Petersburg from New Jersey in 1970 to attend Eckerd College. Just as my grandparents Alice and Charles Isleib never looked back once they relocated in Bradenton in 1959 to live out their remaining decades under a warm sun.

How did we get here? What is it about us—my grandparents

and me—that allowed us to slip loose so easily from the northern New Jersey soils that bred us, the family left behind, the
communities, the familiars? Was it Florida that seduced us or
New Jersey that let us go? Is it, was it, a failure of our own
ability to stay in place, a rent in our spirits, or might we have
been drawn here for some necessary purpose?

It's not so much of a problem that we want to come and
embrace this place; it's how we do it, how it's done for us. For
so much of Florida is built on the dead: the killed bays, the
razed scrublands, the buried-alive gopher tortoises. We must
close our eyes to loss in order to live orderly, guilt-free lives in
these places. We assume the best, believe the cheerful corporate
literature. We are pleased with the descriptive names for our
streets and malls and subdivisions: the Oaks Mall (trees cut
down); Turkey Run (turkeys gone), and so forth. We are guilty
first of ignorance, second of strong self-preservation instincts,
third of laziness; the land and its wild creatures always lose
under this scenario.

Since we have not balanced growth and development with
the carrying capacity and unique character of Florida, our public lands are increasingly pressed, loaded with the burden of
being all we have of nature. It is as if I were to say: the skin on
my arms alone will have to perform all the functions my entire
body's skin once did. All feeling must come through my arms,
all sensation, all caress, all oxygen exchange, all function of
skin. Only here can the sunshine, or the wind, touch me.

In my parents' minds, there was never a question about
my going to college, about the essential path of higher education. They had been both scarred and energized by the desperate depression-era poverty of their own parents and had
scrabbled hard to gain a toehold on material security. They had
determined never to do without again and to raise a big family
as quickly as possible, just as their friends were doing. All of
this they managed, building security for me and my sisters and

brother, eventually battling high into the middle class, into a security that they hoped would hold. That safety net, they believed, was education.

But my mother never imagined I would move so far away. She lobbied for Douglas College, sister to Rutgers, less than an hour's drive from home. As I pored over college catalogs I'd ordered, circling names that sounded remote and full of possibility, she drew a fast line at the Mississippi River and refused to consider my fantasy of studying oceanography in Hawaii or California. Florida became our compromise. My father's parents had retired to Bradenton on the Gulf Coast, and we all loved the crates of oranges and grapefruits they shipped north every Christmas and the astonishing reports of temperatures in the sixties and seventies when New Jersey's winter snows and short, dark days seemed unwilling ever to give way. Florida became my home.

When the time came, my parents drove me to college, all the way south through the Carolinas and Georgia. In the back seat of the family station wagon, I curled up around the college catalog, and my acceptance letter, and an introductory note from my assigned roommate. On the roof of the car my father had strapped a trunk of my clothes, a jewelry box, an umbrella. Once we arrived in St. Petersburg, I could hardly wait for my parents to leave, so that my new independent life could begin on that wide-open campus by the Gulf of Mexico. My sister told me—years later—of the sorrow pent up in the northbound family station wagon, my mother's suffering over the loss of her first born transmuted into silent grief, the remaining three restless in the back seat, now balancing at the edge of the nest themselves.

"Where you from?" asked a sunburned, yellow-haired boy I hadn't yet seen on campus. He wore a clean white shirt rolled up to his elbows and looked older than the freshman boys I'd seen moving into the dorm adjoining my own.

"Let me guess." He paused dramatically, stepped back, looked me up and down. My face burned under his scrutiny. "With that tan and blonde hair . . . you're from California, right? You're a California girl!" He smiled confidently, moving in close. "Hey, my name's Donny, and I'd say this is my lucky night." Even though his nonstop banter was impossibly trivial, I was flattered to be singled out so quickly from the crowd of freshman girls clustered around the big cast-iron grill.

It was orientation week, and the college was hosting a cook-out for new students in the dorm parking lot nearest the bay. My new dorm mates and I had dressed in short halter-top dresses and walked across our new college campus to this barbeque in a tight anticipatory knot. The tropical, obsidian night and the influx of freshman girls created the perfect setting for the amorous attentions of upperclass and off-campus men.

"You're a freshman, right? Got a boyfriend back home?"

I began to nod over the icy cup of soda I held between my two hands, but he barreled right past my response.

"Sort of? Well, you're a college girl now, and he's probably far, far away. How about we take a walk out to that bench by the water, and you tell me all about yourself."

I rolled my eyes and shrugged my shoulders at my roommate as the town boy steered me through the crowd, his left hand pressed in the small of my back. It was kind of fun to flirt, to feel so grownup and desirable, and I knew the white sundress I'd sewed at home showed off the summery brown of my skin. In his right hand, Donny held a brown paper bag. I could tell by the alcohol content of his breath that he'd had a head start on the illegal bottle.

At the edge of the parking lot, we stopped to take off our sandals, lining them up side by side where the asphalt ended and the sandy ground began. As we struck out toward the water, he pulled me close against his hip, locked his arm around my waist. I had just met this man, but I went willingly into the picture I thought we created, toward the big moon shimmering down into the gulf, across the wide sandy beach unrolling in our path. I thought of how I'd describe my rich and bold new life to my sister back home, this confident man by my side, but my reverie was shattered by a vicious needling pain in my left foot. I stopped abruptly, leaning into the boy, yelping as I extracted a thorn from my tender heel. Another step, and then two, then another stab in the foot.

"Whatsa matter darling?" he asked, breathing hard, nearly losing his balance as he caught my weight.

"Are there blackberries all the way out here?" I wondered; it didn't seem like the right habitat. The round stickery thing dug into my index finger, and after I brushed it off, I sucked little droplets of blood from the hurt fingertip.

"Don't know," he said, nursing his own set of stickers, considerably less glib than he'd begun.

We stepped out again more cautiously, not sure whether to avoid the small grassy clumps we could just make out in the dark or aim for them, as if they were a series of stepping stones.

"Ouch, ouch, oh shit!" We cried out simultaneously, limping to a stop, leaning clumsily against each other to pull more of the sharp thorns from our feet.

"We can make it, let's go on," he urged. But I thought the romantic bench with the moon and gulf view was impossibly out of reach under the circumstances and maybe not such a great idea after all.

"I'm going back," I said, letting go of this man I didn't even know. "This is ridiculous."

I had never encountered a sandspur growing up in New Jersey. I surely didn't understand that night, or at any point during my four years at that college, the story told by that abundant weed: that the soil beneath our feet was actually raw fill, imported to make land where none had been intended, soil so new and sterile that only the first line of colonizer—this sandspur plant—was able to thrive and produce its spiky seed here, declaring this new frontier its home. I had no way of knowing that the ground my college was built on was only recently productive seagrass bed and mangrove forest of Boca Ciega Bay. This had been a clear water, where a person might swim among the bright lives of sea turtle and sand dollar, jumping mullet and dolphin, winked out in the interest of buildable land. But natural configurations of this sweetly curving water body had been ravaged not so long ago; its sunny seagrass beds had been smothered with gray sand from a deeper, darker place, delivered by a dredge and miles of rigid pipe. Neither I nor anyone was ever intended by the natural design of Boca Ciega Bay to walk dry-footed on this place. The seawall that held this new land in place was simply a cement tightrope over strangled bay bottom.

Nor did any of our biology professors interpret for us the false land on which our college was built. Despite the college's open acres of sand and long arcing boundary with Boca Ciega Bay, every field trip we took to net or seine or botanize had to be held off campus in less disturbed landscapes, where natural things still found the habitat they needed to live. One teacher, George Reid, drove us across Maximo Creek to visit a trove of wild orchids in a small park, a secret remnant of the Florida that had been. He knew that to love a thing you must experience it for yourself, firsthand. He also must have felt he could trust us with the knowledge of those rarities because we were so obviously preoccupied with the emotional adjustments of freshman year.

During the four years that I lived on the Eckerd College campus, I often walked the mile or more of outermost cement seawall that kept the college from the bay. The seawall stood inert, holding back its tons of imported fill dirt for us to live on. I never seriously questioned the absence of shorebirds or marine creatures in the salt water bumping up against the seawall, never had the words to wonder why there wasn't the abundance of life I was used to seeing in my growing years by the Atlantic Ocean.

In the altered landscape of St. Petersburg in the 1970s, there wasn't a chance of seeing a swallow-tailed kite or really very much in the way of natural fauna, and I didn't. A dorm mate from Tennessee signed up for a three-day canoe trip down the Peace River, some miles inland from our college, and returned with reports of butter-yellow prothonotary warblers and incessantly calling red-shouldered hawks and black river currents. Her experience was only words to me then.

Although I didn't come to Florida thirty years ago intending to stay, my grandparents did. They carefully chose subtropical Bradenton as the place to retire, moving into a simple, freshly built two-bedroom pastel yellow ranch home with cedar-lined closets and cool terrazzo floors; tall, louvered windows to catch the breezes; and, most inviting of all, a Florida room, surrounded on three sides by screen. My grandfather replaced his life work as an accountant in New York City with the tending of a quarter acre of coarse St. Augustine grass and a small selection of subtropical citrus.

About once a month, they would set out north across the Sunshine Skyway bridge to my college, just on the other side of Boca Ciega Bay in St. Petersburg, to bring me home for the weekend. On the slow ride back to Bradenton in their immaculate copper sedan, always traveling five miles per hour under the speed limit, I would feel the length of the weekend extending out in front of me, luxurious and interminable in its scripted precision. Grandma would move into Grandpa's narrow, cool bedroom, to a rollaway cot perpendicular to the foot of his single bed. I slept in her room, on a maple twin that matched his. When the door was closed, I would turn over the simple brush and mirror on her dresser in my hands and lift the small silver bowls that held her bobby pins and hairnets. In all the house, the only untidiness was in a small stack of papers on a tray on this dresser, lists and letters and interesting recipes and notes to herself, weighted down with a dog-eared calendar that marked the events not of a single year but of a lifetime, all the births and deaths and anniversaries she wanted to remember. My grandmother and I shared the spacious, mint green–tiled bathroom adjoining the bedrooms. My grandfather, and any other men in the family who visited, were relegated to a tiny, trailer-sized bathroom in the garage (much to my younger brother's indignation). Grandpa placed great store in his personal appearance, shaving carefully each morning before a mirror hung on the back of the bathroom door, holding his elbows close to his ribs to avoid hitting the shower or the medicine cabinet, to his left and right. You couldn't help but be impressed with the order and tidiness of my grandparents' home, celibate, split, the polar opposites separated, the male and the female, the dark and the light. And with its safety.

I stayed in bed as late as I dared those mornings, inhaling the sweet scent of gardenia and listening to the monotonous coo of mourning doves. When I finally rose from my grandmother's bed, my place would be set at the round white breakfast table, a large cup and saucer for instant coffee, a glass of orange juice, a green porcelain bowl for cereal, a toaster at the ready, and two halves of a pink grapefruit just picked from my grandmother's favorite fruit tree. Every morning, my grandparents spooned those astringent grapefruit sections from their own backyard tree into their eager, northern-bred mouths, and so would I, when I visited.

"Nothing better to keep you regular," my grandmother would tell me, but I knew she simply loved the fruit, all on its own.

After breakfast there would be the washing up of the dishes, and then we'd adjourn to the stiffly webbed lounge chairs in the Florida room to read the thin Bradenton paper. And then what? A desperation of time until the next meal's preparation should begin. My grandmother generally planned a short field trip to the beach on Anna Maria Island, nine miles to the west, or to a small park or museum, and she liked to talk to me about current events. They always admired me, my tan and my neat clothes and my slim weight, and liked to hear what I could tell of my small successes at college. But I could not speak of my emotional insufficiencies, or the dark side of the men I dated, or any other form of angst. Nor did they tell me of theirs.

As my grandfather aged, he began slowly to cut back the plantings in their yard. Grandpa had no quarrel with the mannerly branches and tiny orange fruits of the calamondin outside the kitchen window, even though they were rarely eaten. It was the grapefruit tree, sprawling and fecund, lit by perfect yellow globes of pink-fleshed fruit, that distressed him—even though its abundance of fruit fed them each morning from November through April. He began his campaign to control it by lopping off limbs he considered "messy," starting with the one that overhung the invisible line in the St. Augustine grass dividing his yard from his neighbor's. Stooped and fragile, Grandpa would try to lift with thick ropes the branches that he felt hung too low to the ground, or he would prop them with sturdy poles, but the tree didn't easily succumb to his will. Nothing about the grapefruit tree was sedate. Its leaves were huge, lustrous, darkest of green. Grandpa would rake and sweep the ground beneath the tree's deep, shady canopy to raw dirt, and when an overripe fruit at the top of the tree would fall and split, opening untidily to flies and rot, he would cart it off to the shiny aluminum garbage tins outside the garage within the hour.

When my father or his brother, my uncle Donald, would visit, Grandpa would enlist their help, pulling out a saw and wheelbarrow, appealing to them to prune yet another errant branch from the glossy-leaved grapefruit tree. I'd stand close, begging them to go easy, to remember the fabulous winter bounty. Grandpa supervised the amputation, stooped, anxious, and insistent. After dinner, he would study the limbed-up tree from his lounge chair in the Florida room, relaxing as the tree came to more closely resemble the safely reduced image he had in his mind.

One time I came back to find the tree entirely gone save for a shorn stump ringed by carefully raked sand. No mess. No grapefruit. I don't remember what my grandmother said, whether she spoke about it at all.

The next morning, over coffee, Grandpa pushed an ad across the table that he'd clipped from the Sunday newspaper supplement: "A wonder plant, a miraculous type of lavender, a plant for all seasons and climates and soils, for all gardeners . . . Will be sent to you by parcel post for only $19.95, guaranteed to thrive anywhere in the continental U.S." A tiny flare must have illuminated in what remained of his once considerable gardener's imagination.

"What do you think?" he asked. "I'd like to put this lavender in the planters out front. Do you think it will do well here?"

"Don't know, Grandpa," I shrugged. "Maybe." The only plant that had really interested me in his manicured lawn was gone. After I returned to school, and while the hothouse lavender plants traveled to him from some faraway greenhouse, he tore up the luxuriant plantings of cape jasmine in the planters under the bedroom window and filled them with rich, loosened soil, preparing to pamper those generic hothouse babies when they arrived. But the damp heat of south Florida was not in the planting zone favored by lavender, after all, and he eventually replaced their quickly dwindled corpses with smooth white pebbles that came in a heavy-gauge plastic bag from the hardware store.

Searching for Swallow-tails

It was an emphatic ninety-eight degrees on the first day of June, when I met up once again with Dr. Ken Meyer and his field crew in southwest Florida's Big Cypress National Preserve. That didn't include what the crew's tree climber, Megan Parker, termed the "phenomenal humidity" spun our way by the year's first hurricane shaping up over Cuba. The kites had hatched what young they could this season, and those chicks were almost ready to leave their nests. Ken and his team were working every hour of the long summer daylight to study and mark the adolescent birds.

The crew, consisting of Ken, Megan, and two technicians, Deb Duvall and John Arnett, had begun work before sunrise and had already outfitted two kite chicks with radio transmitters when I met them at noon. Now they were schlepping climbing gear, toolbox, water, and a heavy plastic duffel fifteen minutes down a winding trail to a slash pine topped by the third kite nest on the day's agenda. I fell in eagerly behind them on the rough-trodden trail. Two, six, ten, then sixteen agitated adult swallow-tailed kites circled the tree, calling urgently, confirming that we were in the right place. The nest looked to be about sixty-five feet off the ground, wedged among the topmost branches of a loblolly pine tree.

"This is a damn nice tree—something that can actually support my weight," joked Megan, a lanky field tech who had just arrived from Idaho to assist Ken with the tree climbing. "It's a big tree, compared to the garbage Ken's been showing me!"

Despite the presence of the anxious adult kites, an almost sure sign that young were on the nest, the team's first task was to confirm that the young bird was actually there. No one could spot the chick with binoculars.

"Nest looks a little rough around the edges," said Ken.

Megan and Deb scouted the underbrush, turning up feathers, fragments of a wasp nest (a major food item brought to the young birds by their parents from the surrounding forest), and fresh "whitewash" on the ground. All good signs, everyone agreed.

But within less than a minute of our arrival, they also located a dead kite chick, tangled in the underbrush at the base of the nest tree. Ants crowded the bird's eyeballs and swarmed the length of its frail wing bones.

"It's only four weeks old," Ken said, gently fingering the small corpse. Its white, almost translucent feet and beak hung limp and bleached with death. "It would not have left the nest on its own for at least another week."

Ken kicked up downed nest material around the base of the tree. It wasn't much to see: pencil-thin pine branchlets, pale lichens, and a greenish curly relative of Spanish moss. High wind is the number one killer of nestling kites, Ken told me, and from the location of the twigs and the condition of the bird, he was almost positive that the previous night's violent storm knocked this chick from its nest.

"I'm going to sit over here and get depressed," said Ken. "I really thought we'd get this nest." I joined him in the scanty shade of a slash pine. Directly above, a half dozen adult kites planed overhead, repeating their three-part cries: *killy-killy-killy*. I could almost believe that they were trying to call the young one back into life.

After a quick water break, we resumed the struggle through the grapevine and palmetto and scoured the surrounding trees with binoculars, hoping to spot a surviving sibling.

"Just tell us, birds, just tell us," I chanted to the sky. "Have you got another baby out there somewhere? Don't make us work so hard."

"They are telling us," said Ken. "We don't know how to listen well enough."

❧

Field technician John Arnett didn't wait for the birds to talk. When he first located this nest three weeks ago, he suspected there was another nearby. Now he rejoined us, emerging from a nearby stand of pines, a rare grin on his face: "There's another nest over here! And nobody dead under it!"

Unfortunately, no live birds remained in the nest, either. The crew packed up their gear and water bottles and headed for the trucks. Stuffing my tape recorder and notebooks into my day pack, I followed. When I unlocked my car, the metal handle raised a blister on my skin. Visible waves of superheated air poured from the dark blue interior. Everyone agreed it made sense to drive north to Sunniland to stock up on ice and drinks and snacks. As we drove, I pelted Ken with questions, pressing him for more detail about this part of his study.

He said, "The kicker is, we know so little about swallow-tailed kites. We can't even tell male from female without drawing blood or performing surgery. I don't know where the birds go after they fledge or anything about what happens to them on their wintering grounds in South America. But at the rate natural communities are being destroyed here and in the rain forests, I feel some anxiety about what it will take to keep the birds around."

I scribbled notes in the noisy car as we bumped down the lime rock road. I backed up my barely legible notes with a small, battery-powered tape recorder. It seemed so important to get this—everything I was seeing, the persistent orchestration of scientific groundwork—recorded with complete accuracy. Ken's urgency was palpable.

"To acquire the information, the data I need," he continued, "I've got to find sixty nests and radio-tag thirty young birds during this season and the next two. Probably because of the high water all over south Florida, we've had a heck of time finding nests this year. Over the past six years, the average amount of time just to find a single nest was fifteen hours, with a standard deviation of three—that's pretty consistent from year to year. But this year, the average time to simply find one nest was over thirty hours.

"Kites are great birds, but you have to work so hard for the tiniest bits of data. I just have to resign myself to small sample sizes and obscure statistical tests."

I thought to myself: my faith in this man is absolute. If anyone can get the information he is seeking, he will. As I write down his words, take these notes, the anxiety that's been rising inside me quiets.

A thunderstorm began circling in from the south and east. The temperature eased into the low nineties. There remained a 5 p.m. appointment with a nest tree across Highway 29 and south a bit, at the twenty-six-thousand-acre Florida Panther Refuge. The technicians unloaded the climbing gear, rope, five ten-foot sections of aluminum ladder, cameras, and banding equipment and lashed it snug against the roll bar of the refuge's high-tired swamp buggy.

"The fact that things are so quiet makes me doubt the young are still in the nest," said Ken when the refuge personnel showed us their nest. "There should be begging, there should be feeding. I'm inclined to think it failed rather than fledged—no adults close by. If chicks had fledged, they'd most likely still be in the nest or perching somewhere close by."

"One minute more," Debbie asked. "I think I see something light up there."

Megan added: "If I saw something light, it was fuzzy." That, of course, would be the head of a chick. The two women crouched on their haunches, watching for telltale movement in the nest.

But there was nothing up there that any of us could make out.

We spotted a fledged kite with a short tail flapping over the trees as we left the refuge. Its flight was labored. Probably seven weeks old, said Ken. First one he'd seen out of the nest this year.

"The birds are growing as we speak at the other nests we've got marked," Ken fretted, thinking about the next day's agenda.

I was reminded of what he'd explained earlier: almost everything we know about swallow-tailed kites is based on the slender period of time, during breeding season, that they spend in North America. To learn more, Ken had designed a long-term study based on radio-tagging and monitoring sixty-five young birds. The best age for radio-tagging young swallow-tails is around thirty-five days. At this age, about four to six days before they can fly, the birds are large enough to be properly fitted with transmitters but too young to jump from the nest. These biological realities make for a hard-edged window of opportunity that had this crew scrambling all over the southern peninsula of Florida.

We continued back to the field station, driving through a grassy prairie, framed in drifts of soft dwarf cypress, as pretty as any meadow I'd ever seen. Anywhere. Clear pink meadow beauties, jewel-like sundews, and white bog buttons punctuated the marsh grasses. Rosy gold light poured from the flat-bottomed thunderhead rising Himalaya high over Naples, thirty miles to the west. The sky sprawled round as a bowl. Six or eight different cloudscapes dominated as many points of the compass. We stopped the car so we could turn full circle in one place, standing on the ground. The energy of the warm, eighty-seven-degree gulf water built these thunderheads, these Florida mountains, as high as the moon. The wind was steady and, for the first time that day, held a hint of cool. I couldn't have been happier.

Ken instructed the crew to converge at 6 a.m. the next morning for the two-hour drive north to the next nest site, near Avon Park. Unfortunately, there wouldn't be room for me to follow until after lunch, Ken told me. I returned to the staff housing, wondering what to do with myself in the meantime, restless, even frustrated. I had only two days to follow these guys around, and I didn't want to miss a minute of watching what they did. Meanwhile, there was no other way for me to be with the kites. I knew enough about them by now to appreciate how thinly their nests were scattered about the landscape and how unlikely it would be to just "find" one at this time of year.

I settled on the second-floor deck of the technicians' rented house, staring into the wedge of south Florida sky. The warm, wet fullness of the air, so thick, and the rising rapid insect calls, along with the voices of tree frogs, pileated woodpeckers, and red-shouldered hawks, returned me to my gladness simply to be here. I chided myself for my impatience. I thought about all the ways I could imagine to be close to kites and then my corollary question: If I am close enough, will I know how to protect them, to see to their protection? I thought over the strange dichotomy of how the scientists have to handle the birds, surely against the preferences of the animals themselves. I thought about watching Megan hand-stitching a fleece hood for the kite chicks, to keep them calm while she transported them for banding. I thought briefly of my early years as a field technician, after college, and I knew I no longer wanted to be the person who captured the birds, who climbed after them, and handled them.

I began to wonder how I might embrace the bird and learn about it in an entirely different way. I stood, stretching my spine long, imagining what it might feel like to merge my body with that of a swallow-tailed kite. I imagined the wings of the bird entering me, filling my arms with great, light powerful bones, feeling my own bones emptying and becoming spacious, loosening and dropping the hard-won calcium that I would need to sustain upright posture through my old age. Deliberately, I let that mineral go. I felt all my power gathered in my wing-arms, and my split-fork tail, and my eagle-sharp eyes. I could feel the prick of ten thousand feather shafts piercing through my skin from the inside of my body out, how they would be snow white and ebony and, on my back, steely blue. And then, I pictured myself dropping from the height of this porch, finding a shelf of the wind, sensing every mood of that element, its tiniest intent.

The breath of the wind is my breath, I thought. No, the wind blows through me, through the newly emptied spaces of my bones; it possesses me, it is me, just as the bird has passed into me. I imagined letting go into the wind. I became sensation, no conscious thought. I climbed the shaft of the wind because I could, because it was mine to do. I just cleared the treetops, tilting over the intimate hiding places of tree snakes and green frogs. As I belonged to the wind, so these belonged to me.

Mosquitoes buzzing and biting returned me from my reverie. Kites seemed so opposite from me, I thought. I am grounded, heavy bodied, and stiff in comparison, rarely moved by the wind. My life and my thoughts are complex and car-bound. My relationships are equally complex and highly charged and at the same time too static. So unlike me, the kite moves through its living without forethought, completely present in each moment. My body memory does propel me, like the kite, but to do that traveling, I wear down rubber tires and burn fossil fuel. I leave my child in the care of others. I pause in the earning of money. My garden grows weeds. I miss the cucumber harvest altogether. Wouldn't it make more sense to watch the kite from just one place, to take it where it comes to me? What is this thing in me that always wants more, wants to seek and find the kite on its own ground, to learn more than is freely given?

One way I have found the things I urgently seek, or want to know, is to follow the groundwork of other people, to piggy-back on the work of experts, just as I am here to observe what Ken and his crew are doing. In a sense I purloin their effort and hard work.

Who am I, then, this watcher? Am I simply here to transcribe, as I had thought when I first made contact with Ken, as I believe I have prepared myself to do? Moreover, I wonder, do our scientists, even the very best of them, know all the questions we need to be asking ourselves about sustaining life on this planet? And do they hold as well the only methods there are to gain the answers?

When the call came to rejoin the kite crew, I put aside my musings and picked up my notebook and tape recorder. Things were looking up in the field. John Arnett had located an active nest, with a live chick inside. And Megan had nothing but praise for the tree's ample sturdiness ("God forbid something should have that diameter!" she crowed.)

So far, so good. The task now was to get a climbing rope for Megan over a major limb in roughly the middle third of the crown of the tree. Ken knotted a lead egg sinker to heavy monofilament line loaded on a Mitchell spinning reel. He slipped the dull gray sinker into the leather basket of a wrist rocket slingshot, which he supported on his left forearm.

Over and over, Ken zinged the sinker skyward. Again and again, it fell short or tangled in a thick bit of foliage. The technicians took their turns when Ken's wrist got sore.

"This isn't going to work," Ken said, fifty minutes and innumerable shots later. "We're wasting a lot of energy going horizontally. Maybe we should bag it." This is what he said, but what he did was figure out another way to get a rope up the towering pine. He switched to the next weapon in his arsenal, the dummy launcher, a sort of dull gun made by marine supply companies to shoot line between boats. The launcher, powered by a .22 shell, is also used to train retriever dogs, someone told me. The launcher had plenty of power but was extremely noisy, and its aim was crude.

Boom! I covered my ears too late.

Boom! Over and over, the big red dummy shot from the

launcher and hung up tight as a pine cone on improbable branches, never where it seemed to be aimed and sometimes alarmingly close to the nest.

Boom!

"Somebody else want to do this?" offered technician Arnett. "I'm almost permanently deaf."

Deb returned to the truck for earplugs and more line, and Ken took over the firing.

"Let's see how long we can make this take," said Ken, only half joking, taking stock of the lowering sky. Three hours had passed since we began tackling this tree. Ken polled his crew, and they deliberated, weighing the time they could spend on this nest against the likelihood of an approaching storm. They allotted themselves three more shots with the crude launcher.

I found myself intensely wishing I could help, that somehow I could contribute to their effort, engage more concretely with the work at hand. I tried to write down everything the crew said and did because telling their story was my job on this trip. But I felt like something of a voyeur.

What have I ever done with this much sustained focus? I wondered.

"Actually, I believe I'm getting a little more consistent," said Ken, considering the placement of his twelfth shot. "What do you think about that one?" He addressed his question to Megan. It was her weight, after all, that the branch needed to bear.

Megan trained her binoculars on the tree, trying to pick out the trajectory of the thin glistening line.

"Oh, I see it, I see it!" she said. "My feeling is . . ."

Ken groaned: "Whenever she starts with 'my feeling,' it's not going to be any good."

Megan reassured him: "The limb that it's over is fine if we can just move it closer to the trunk."

Somehow Ken did, and the crew shifted into action. With

heavy silver duct tape, they fastened the end of the monofilament to white clothesline, then tied on the blue climbing rope. The adult birds had resumed their vigil, calling, circling, full of concern. Megan guessed that, to them, there was something very predatorlike about the colorful ropes snaking up the tree.

Thunder grumbled closer.

Ken wrapped the climbing rope three times around the thick-based pine and secured it tight with a bowline and two clove hitches. I thought it was a beautiful rope, azure crisscrossed with green fibers and a dash of hot pink.

"Are we worried about the thunder?" someone murmured. Again, the crew deferred to the climber.

"I'm happy to go but I don't know what we're expecting here in terms of weather. I'm not afraid of it, but I want to use some judgment," considered Megan, studying the movement of the wind in the tops of the pine trees. "I kind of want to go because we've rigged it."

The storm decided otherwise. Gusting wind shook free a torrent of rain and nailed it down with a convincing bolt of lightning. We sprinted back to the oaks, hunkering under a plastic blue tarp spread over the bed of the truck. While we waited, I turned to Megan, who held a corner of the tarp over her lightly built, six-foot frame. Her thin blue T-shirt had darkened, absorbing rainwater from her thick, sun-bleached braid. How did she come to be a climber of raptor nests?

"Some years back I got hired by the Peregrine Fund to study laughing falcons and bat falcons in Guatemala," she told me. "I knew I was going to be climbing trees, so I had a friend rig a twenty-foot climbing rope in a tree in my yard. It seemed so high and so complicated. All those knots. Once I got there, I had to climb these huge trees, maybe ninety feet tall, every day. There was no one around to spot or coach. Just me and a Guatemalan, before light, pantomiming. When you are so naive, one thing isn't worse than another. But it was a real macho thing. I was the only woman. I wasn't about to complain. There was a lot of up and down, making all the mistakes you can think of, without an audience. They would nail sticks together to make a ladder a hundred feet up. I would never do that again without protection.

"But after a while it became the most comforting thing in the world to be up there five or six hours a day. The trees twist through every dimension, with these big comfortable branches. It seemed sort of womblike up there. And every tree had its own definite personality. You wouldn't believe what I saw from up there: troops of monkeys, incredible hummingbirds, neat insects."

Megan completed her thesis on laughing falcons in Guatemala and moved to Stanley, Idaho, where she studies wolf pack vocalizations. Her home is a nylon canvas yurt ("the size of a closet") near the spectacular Sawtooth Wilderness; two dogs and Polarfleece sheets keep her warm through the minus-forty-degree winter nights. It's the stuff of woodswomen fantasies—mine, anyway.

Finally, the rains let up. Megan pulled her purple climbing harness over her hips and adjusted the brightly colored mechanical ascenders fitted and tied to her height and stride. Suddenly she hung free, five feet off the ground and about that same distance from the trunk of the eighty-foot tree. She paused to adjust a knot. She kicked up the rope so fluidly and effortlessly that I was hardly aware of the technical competence, the daring, the balance, the physical strength all bound up in this single upward movement. For the next five minutes, the only sound I heard was her breathing, heavy and audible. Bits of bark dislodged from the tree and drifted over us. The attending adult kites called shrilly, once again highly agitated by Megan's approach. She slung a piece of red webbing over the branch supporting the climbing rope, pulled her body up, tied on to the main trunk with a safety rope.

"This makes me *so* nervous," said Ken, almost a prayer.

Megan tied and retied protection anchors above her body,

moving steadily toward the dinner-plate-sized nest. None of us could take our eyes off the climber, as if we might will her safe through our undivided attention.

I remembered something she had told me under the rain fly: "Climbing has got more to do with rhythm than strength. It's just basically climbing a ladder. That's all there is, but you can fight it, and then it takes a tremendous amount of strength. What I do is get totally focused and quiet and just blast up. The hardest thing is balancing up there while you're waiting for the bird to come back up."

Watching Megan, I felt so sedentary, so physically slack. I thought about what I had observed of the technicians' lives the night before, overhearing their conversations. I thought of how John Arnett had rolled his eyes at Ken's 11 p.m. reminder call about some gear requirement, after a fourteen-hour day in the field, but how they all still rose, uncomplaining, at 5:30 a.m., to begin again. How they rarely take days off during the field season, adjusting their lives to the frenetic pace of the birds' nesting, the short window of opportunity available to collect all that Ken needs to know. I thought of how sparse and temporary the quarters of field biologists generally seem and how rarely a settled dinner, a stable relationship, or a predictable life routine figured into their lives. It had been twenty years and twenty pounds since this had been my life. It still fascinated me, but I'd lost the requisite toughness somewhere along the way.

"Here comes the wind," said Deb and Ken simultaneously. We felt the prefacing breeze of storm on our skin.

And then we saw big wings, kite wings, held unnaturally stiff against the gray sky. Megan had the half-grown chick by the feet. Carefully she slid it into an orange cloth sack.

Ken let out a long breath and all the pent-up praise and encouragement he'd been holding inside: "You did a great job, Megan. I thought you had many feet to climb yet. You're the best—that was just great."

I, too, was overwhelmed by all that I had seen so far. I felt secure in Ken's science, his careful precautions, his team's dedication, Megan's competence.

Megan sent the bag quickly down the rope. "I'd sure appreciate as much speed as possible," she called. "I'm about to get a haircut from one of these parents." We could see and hear the fluttering commotion of the adults, about eight feet above her head.

The technicians arranged a simple work space on a green waterproof ground cloth under the tree. Ken taught his "techs" as he worked.

"Okay, the way I get him out of the bag is I feel for the head. I'm going to try to reach in and get hold of one of his shoulders. You peel the bag back, contain the feet. Don't want to pull the toes too hard, you can damage them."

The ungainly chick, with its brown speckled head and chest, had none of the sleek elegance of the adult swallow-tailed kite. It still clutched pine branchlets from its nest in its talons. I thought about the twiggy nests in these tallest of trees, how tightly these birds must cling to such sparse support from the moment they hatch.

Deb slipped a soft, green, hand-stitched hood over the bird's head to calm it. Then the bird was weighed: 505 grams, the second heaviest so far, said Ken. He measured the feet and bill, then bent a silver identification band around the bird's leg.

Now the bird was cradled on its back in Deb's hands.

"Fast heartbeat, Deb?" asked Ken. He knew she loved this intimacy with the kites.

She nodded yes. "Mine, too."

The chick barely moved in her hands. But its thin, piteous cries through the hood seemed to stimulate an intensified response from the attending adults far above. It was hard to listen to them.

Ken and John fitted the bird with a backpack harness holding a radio transmitter. Ken had showed me the transmitter the night before: the world's tiniest, not much larger than an AA battery, weighing only eighteen grams. So tiny it had to be assembled under a microscope.

And expensive. This single transmitter cost nearly $3,000. The more common radio transmitters, which enabled Ken to locate birds within a few miles using a hand-held antenna, cost only $150. But these new transmitters, linked to a satellite orbiting more than five hundred miles above the earth's surface, would allow Ken to track his birds planetwide wherever they might go.

The bird struggled as the soft Teflon ribbon harness slipped over each wing. Nothing in its young life had prepared it for this experience. Ken centered a square of soft material on the bird's sternum, the deliberately weak link in the harness. Here, cotton attachment threads would slowly rot and weaken through wear and exposure during the two-to-five-year life span of the tiny transmitter on the bird's back, eventually allowing it to fall free.

"I haven't checked the right cable wrap, but the left is great," Ken reported. He used pliers to snug the harness, then superglued the transmitter in place. "I want to leave a certain amount of play because the bird is still growing; even if it were fully grown, you'd leave a little bit of slack."

"I'm not having much fun up here," Megan reminded us from the tossing treetop.

"We're almost done, Meg," Ken reassured. He checked his watch, frowned. "Twenty minutes. I promised her fifteen." For the moment, the adults had swung far away into the stormy sky. The absence of their cries was a relief.

Now, the last step, the most intrusive. A kite's sex organs are internal, so it's impossible to tell a male from a female until it mates. This year, a colleague of Ken's in Miami had offered to sex the birds based on blood samples obtained in the field.

"Put its head at my two o'clock," Ken instructed Deb. She

extended the wing and held it in place so Ken could withdraw a tiny sample of its blood. I was asked to hold the wing tip—my first real job. Three tiny bird mites scurried up my arm. There was no sound from the chick, although its chest heaved as the needle entered a prominent vein. Drops of sweat rolled off Ken's forehead and mingled with bits of white feather shaft on the green plastic drop cloth. Then it was over. John labeled the tiny tube: "STK 10."

Ken looked up at the sky. Lightning traced closer, through the pine forest. "We're done, Megan. We're just waiting for the puncture to heal, and we'll have him back up.

"Okay, I'm putting him in the bag. If you'll just check its wing to make sure it's not bleeding when you get it."

"Sure," Megan said. She hauled the bright cotton bag up against the gray sky and then out of our sight. A cool rain began as Megan rappelled down the brilliant rope. I could see how she'd wrapped the rope around her leg as a break, controlling the speed of her swift descent with a leather glove on her right hand. Faces upturned, we watched her. Rain fell into our eyes, rain from far higher than the nest and the young bird, from higher even than the adult kites that now hung noiseless in the sky.

I said my farewells and climbed back into my car, lowering the windows to shoo out an eager cotillion of mosquitoes. The south Florida landscape whizzed past my windshield as I accelerated once again to the speed of ordinary life, hurrying north to child and work. I really hated to leave—I knew it'd be hard to redefine my life outside kites again. My mind was filled with all that I'd witnessed, and I wondered where my travels with Ken and the birds might take me next. If I could see everything there was to see about kites, close up, by following Ken and absorbing everything he knows, then the puzzle pieces to this question—What will it take to keep kites surviving in Florida?—might fall into place.

Down at the breaking edge of the continent, where dry lime rock edged into salt water south of Everglades City, I felt immense possibility, all of Florida and the whole of my life, spread out in my northbound path. I thought of how the kites disperse themselves in the same direction, settling into what territories they will, just as I was moving into the territory of knowing them.

And I thought how curious it had been to notice myself so singularly as an observer: Would it be possible, ever, I wondered, to integrate the role of reporting with being in the story? Could I learn to bring these lives I was living—home and wild—so disparate—into a single life that fully satisfied and didn't leave anything I wanted behind?

Wood Ducks

Twenty years earlier, under a hot May sun, I stood at a small kiosk outside the biology department offices, paging through layers of announcements for graduate programs and summer jobs. Sweat collected in the hollow of my back. In just a month, I'd graduate. As a child, I had set my career compass on biology, immersing myself in the early writings of Rachel Carson. I wanted to become something I could best describe as a "forest conservationist." I imagined myself as a sort of shepherd of trees, that I would see to their growing; a career taking care of something worthy, a grown-up version of babysitting or waitressing, a concrete, doable job. Now I thought I might pursue graduate school in genetics because my major professor was funny and gentle, a superb teacher who seemed actually to see me as a person, even a person with some promise. But the list of graduate courses in human genetics on these flyers made me yawn.

A hot wind riffled the pages of possible jobs and schooling, lifted their bottom edges off the corkboard. Now here was something different: a fall internship at the Savannah River Ecology Laboratory in Aiken, South Carolina. The job was field biology; it offered a small salary, and it sounded like real work. I was hungry for all three. I had so wondered how I would come to do actual conservation: no one had mentioned that word in my four years of undergraduate academics. The words on that flyer elicited a flicker of excitement in my belly. I filled out the application form and mailed it to the lab that same afternoon.

Three months later, after graduation and a last summer at the beach, I moved north to Aiken, South Carolina. Still within the range of the swallow-tailed kite; in fact, it was there that I first saw the bird.

My first assignment was to grind frozen samples of cattail

stem and run them through a lengthy procedure called electrophoresis to determine the plants' relationship to one another. As I sat in the cramped lab, titrating chemicals and washing glassware, I kept the door half open so I could watch and intercept other field station employees passing by who were generally headed for more exciting outdoor destinations. Late afternoons and weekends, I was free to venture out with whichever researchers would take me along. A sleek blonde woman named Karen taught me how to run a johnboat and a drift fence; tall, swarthy Tom Murphy let me tag along on thrilling nighttime alligator captures; and many nights I joined a group of graduate students who roved the deserted blacktop roads of the Savannah River Plant, catching snakes on the road at night from the rolling van. When we'd spot a rope's length of black racer or oak snake in our headlights, the herpetology students would throw themselves from the vehicle, trying to pin down and bag the snake before it recovered from the blinding lights; I'd try to feel my way to the driver's seat to hit the brakes before the van veered into a ditch.

One particularly tedious afternoon in the lab, a thickly bearded man stuck his head in the doorway to make my acquaintance.

"Hey," he said. His nut-brown eyes looked friendly, though I couldn't tell if he was really smiling behind that thick shrubbery of facial hair.

"What do you do?" I blurted, always looking for an outing.

"Oh, I'm just an old swamp rat," he said, explaining nothing and everything. "You want to see the swamp, meet me in the lab parking lot at 5:30. Rustle up a pair of chest waders and don't be late."

That evening, we drove more than an hour south and east toward the great Savannah River swamp, first on hard-paved roads, then dirt, finally bumping down a mere track between the trees. We hiked through the darkening woods, carrying shotguns on our shoulders, to the edge of the upland forest. We

climbed into his elevated wooden tree stand, really just a narrow platform of two-by-fours, in the last of the light of the day.
That night, and others, our job was simply to tally numbers of
wood ducks as they coasted to roost with thin whistling squeals
in the nearby wooded slough. Between incoming rafts of ducks,
the swamp rat taught me to tell the up-and-down flight of red-
winged blackbirds from the straight arrowing of mourning
doves, easy once you know how but not if you've never been
shown.

I felt fully alive, sitting on that tree stand, pressed up against
a warm man drinking hot black coffee laced with Southern
Comfort, waiting for wood ducks. It was the most exciting thing
I'd ever done. Sometimes the evenings would involve shooting
a half dozen ducks for his dissertation. He insisted that I learn to
shoot the gun at the ducks myself. I didn't like the thought of
killing the ducks or the gun's rough kick against my shoulder,
but it was so dark that I couldn't make the visual connection
between the shell that I let fly and its actual penetration into the
wild animal's body. And besides, the ducks never made a sound;
all I could hear was the Halloween wind in the cypress trees and
the barely audible wing beats of bats, circling, and the fearful
hammer of my heart. I preferred sliding down the tree and into
the water to retrieve the warm limp bodies the duck man had
shot. Pushing through the chill swamp in chest-high waders, I
felt completely embodied, loving the weighted press of the deep
water against my belly and thighs. I was happy to follow his
lead in all things, cultivating in myself a powerful love for wild
southern landscapes. The certain but unseen alligators and water moccasins in the waist-deep water in which I waded were an
acceptable edge, a risk I agreed to bear, or ignore, for the privilege of being there. He had told me the truth: he was a swamp
rat. He loved mentoring the eager, young (blonde) college students who passed through the lab's internship program—just
like me. In fact, there were clones of us, I found out later, perhaps even generations. At the time, none of the price tags hung

on that way of being in the wild ever seemed too high, not even the unremarkable coupling in a run-down field trailer that sometimes followed our time on the tree stand. He was my ticket to the nighttime wilderness. If this was the life of a field biologist, I wanted to be counted in.

Other evenings after work, I would sit with my friends on one or another of our rough-screened porches, focusing my first pair of binoculars on a feeder just outside. Number one: a small noisy creature with an ebony cap and throat. A chickadee, of course: hadn't I known this bird all my life? But my new bird list asked: Is it the black-capped or Carolina version? I had to learn the difference, and as I did, I marked off that chickadee on a folded paper checklist of the birds of South Carolina.

Winter delivered brilliant cardinals, startling evening grosbeaks, and blazing yellow goldfinches to the sunflower seeds we provided. Check. Check. Check. The simple marks meant I was there. I had seen these miracles, this was my response. We would circle the total number of a day's sightings at the top of the list, counting and recounting. Thirty kinds of birds, then forty. I wanted to find more. Flipping through Peterson's *Field Guide to the Birds*, I noticed its organization by families containing similar, related species. If I could locate all the ducks commonly occurring in South Carolina, I could add twenty or more checks to my list.

A co-worker left a guide to the water birds of North America on my desk with a small note affixed: "Learn!" And so I made my way through the ducks that first winter, squinting to distinguish their profiles in flight against the lowering sky of the coastal marshes and memorizing the distinctive plumages of male and female where they differed. Common loon. Red-breasted and hooded mergansers. Blue-winged teal. My favorite: the shoveler, with its comical spatulate bill.

On weekends, we stalked the circumferences of berry-laden wax myrtles, checking off yellow-rumped warblers and

ruby-crowned kinglets. Over the fields we learned to pick out
the tilt of the wintering marsh hawks, and on the telephone
wires, the kestrels. Each a part of my newly adopted southern
landscape. Each as if it had never before existed. Or maybe it
was my eyes that had just suddenly focused. Where had I been
looking all my life?

Now, on my first Christmas Bird Count in Aiken State Park,
I tallied flocks of American robins in the bitterly cold swamps.
According to the park's bird list, robins occurred here only
from November through March. I had seen plenty of robins
growing up in the north but thought of them only as simple
worm pullers in suburban yards, never before in context: as
members of the thrush family, seasonal travelers through time
and space, deserving of the highest order of awe.

As the seasons turned, with my companions I crossed and
recrossed the rivers of the coastal plain, the Edisto, the
Combahee, the Savannah, listing and checking off not only the
birds but trees, rare flowers, bog-dwelling pitcher plants, and
orchids. Always, we found that someone had traveled these
remote rural spaces before us, naming the plants and birds of
each county. We added their books to the crate of traveling
references in the back of the car: Sprunt and Chamberlain's
South Carolina Bird Life, Radford's *Flora of the Carolinas*, and
simpler, pictorial wildflower keys. Once named, the fallow fields
leaped into sharp relief, no longer anonymous blurs of color but
stands of tiny, cornflower-blue toadflax and coarse, rosy heads
of sheep sorrel, mixing like a palette by Monet. I came to count
on their annual emergence in the resting fields along our route
to the coast, with brilliant phlox and verbena at their feet. In the
same way, we learned to anticipate the black-throated blue warbler and the common redstart and put ourselves in the path of
their northbound migrations in April or early May, noting from
the range map that they travel back every year from the tropics
to breed farther north. In the rainy spring, we apprenticed to
the forest's mushrooms. The guidebooks instructed us to snap

off their fleshy caps and lay them on white paper overnight. By morning, each cap had shaken down a mandala of color, writing for us its individual name in the drift of spoor from its delicate gills.

I was possessed with the abundance of what I saw, the numbers, and the numbers of kinds, and felt no sense of immediate threat to the animals and plants we so happily cataloged and observed. It was a crash course in the most essential kind of sight, the beginning of looking for things within their proper context, coming to see how life weaves into a particular landscape. Our lists began to coalesce as we groped into an understanding that birds occupied particular places or habitats, at most particular times.

As my internship at the lab drew to a close, I asked the wood duck biologist to help me figure out a way to keep doing his kind of work, to keep me outdoors, in the swamp. At that time, no one needed a technician to do the things I had learned to love, so it seemed reasonable to dream up a project for a master's degree. I never thought about how I'd get the course work done. I just wanted an immediate reason to stay outside with the birds.

The wood duck man's major professor at the University of Georgia in Athens remembered a half-finished project he had stored in one of the enormous freezers at the lab. He was happy to hand it over to me. The professor would allow me to fill in the answers to an obscure research question he had asked himself some years back. The question was this: How does the ratio of fat to muscle change in a wood duck's body as it grows? The existing data points were dead young wood ducks, plastic-wrapped in a bank of humming freezers, mixed with hundreds of other researchers' samples collected on the Savannah River Plant. The final, complete data set required ten dead ducks in the freezer for every week of age, between hatchling and ten weeks old. So far, about thirty of the requisite ducks, mostly at the youngest stages, had been collected and frozen. My job was to hatch and rear the rest of the data points, these wildest of ducks.

First, I had to collect wood duck eggs from tall wooden nest boxes that had been nailed high on the trunks of cypress trees all over the plant, miles apart. I climbed each tree by means of shoddily nailed boards, pulled out the eggs, placed them carefully in plastic cartons, edged back down the makeshift ladders, and drove them back to the lab. The relaxed pace of the fall nights was gone. Female ducks were all on the same timetable: mating usually takes place early in March, and most egg laying is complete by April's end. Back at the lab, I set the eggs carefully in a huge steel incubator that occupied the length of a small windowless room.

Weeks later, on Easter morning, the first duckling began to pip out of its shell. I was elated, watching the tiny network of cracks give way to a tiny wet beak chiseling its way into its life. But once the duckling had pipped out of its shell, it launched wild as a tightly wound spring from the incubator, peeping fast and damp and single-minded around that cold linoleum floor, searching in vain for a wildness that room didn't contain. Any thoughts I had of cupping a cute duckling in my hand evaporated as I tried to corner the frantic baby and secure it in a holding pen outside the lab.

To the caged ducklings, I was not the benevolent bringer of food and water, a lover of wild things and their home swamp. I was death. My biggest problem quickly crystallized. Between me and the completion of the professor's data set lay the life of each growing and wary young duck. To answer his question, someone—me, the would-be graduate student—would have to kill each duckling at its appointed time. I never really asked myself why, didn't closely question the value of the study. I knew only that this was a route toward some kind of career in wildlife biology, so I narrowed my focus on the how, not the why.

The wood duck man told me to climb into that muddy pen, slippery with duck feces, single out which animal was the right age by the colored band on its ankle, snag it from its frantic racing around the pen, and then simply strangle it or slam its head against something hard. The swamp man wouldn't do it for me. This was my rite of passage. I got in the pen with the band of desperately peeping ducklings, feathers slick with excrement and fear, but I simply could not kill.

I cajoled a friend to search out some ether for me from the lab's locked chemical cabinet. I thought that anesthetizing the animal would be an easier way for it to die, softer somehow, but young wild things struggle hard against death in any form. In the end it was probably crueler to force the terrified animals into an enormous plastic bag stuffed with chemical-laced cotton. The muted struggle against death seemed just as gruesome. I suppose for me it was easier—the ether was the intermediary—it wasn't my hands, directly, that made the ducks finally go limp. Still, in the end, I managed to kill only a few. Ducks began to escape my makeshift, badly constructed pen. Sometimes I'd come to feed the ducks in the morning and find one or two dead, feathers scattered, a hole dug under the fence by fox or possum. The project began to peter out—there weren't enough ducks for all the missing data points, and we had run out of eggs in the incubator. There would be no more wild-laid eggs that season to fuel the study, and my distaste for my complicity in this project reached such proportions that I finally violated the rules of science and any chance for further "study" with the professor from the university.

One Friday afternoon, I waited until the main parking lot had emptied of employees' cars. I started up one of the lab's pickup trucks and drove it close to the outdoor pen where I'd reared my ducks. I let myself into the muddy pen, and, for the last time, I took up a worn old broom and shooed the wild-eyed, mostly grown ducks into a wire carrying cage.

"Come on, you, I'm trying to save your life," I spoke impa-

tiently to a young male paddling and paddling around the perimeter of the pen, refusing to join the others in the smaller
cage. There was nothing attractive about this young animal's
fear or my own rough handling of the situation. I prodded that
last duck into the crate and trucked the birds secretly to the river
swamp where I'd first fallen in love with their kind. I lowered
the tailgate, opened the crate's wire door and let them go. Even
as they made their way out of the cage, and finally winged their
way into all that freedom, I felt the moment was tainted, for I
had the indecent deaths of their siblings on my hands. I won't
say that I was too squeamish to kill, though I want to. But I
wasn't taught how to administer a respectful death, and I didn't
figure it out on my own. In the end, I took only an indirect
stand, releasing those last wild birds in secret, and I shifted my
career path back to an indoor lab.

In all this time, I never asked myself how I might seek and
connect with wild things on my own terms. Nor this: How I
might more directly serve the wildness I craved.

Unremembered Wings

Near my home in north Florida, almost any sunny day I can look up at the sky and watch the clear air take form: turkey and black vultures, wood storks, a red-shouldered hawk, occasionally a bald eagle join together as morning warms to noon, describing with their bodies otherwise invisible bubbles of warm air, called thermals, that rise off the land. Air blends with bird, and bird with air, individuals, then a whole thing, a continuous reforming. When birds rise and circle in this way, biologists call the phenomenon a "kettle." Thick at the bottom with dark bird bodies, a kettle may spiral up a thousand feet or more, rising like the summer's cumulus—the birds slanting, gliding, belly shining white, the steel-blue glint of a back, dozens of birds, rising on the thermal, defining it, like steam from a tea kettle.

But neither knowing the science nor watching other birds in thermals on a daily basis prepared me for the sight of a thousand swallow-tailed kites surging into the updrafts at the big premigration roost near Lake Okeechobee four summers ago. I climbed from the truck, backed down onto the roughly mown bahia grass, and stared. Among the closest birds I could almost feel the push and spring of muscle against the lifting, heated air and, in some small way, the intimate relationship of kites with the atmosphere of the earth. Too quickly, the highest birds lost the individual precision of their forms and disappeared into illusion—or air.

As our truck rattled down the dike to the remote field site near Fort Center earlier that morning, Ken told me his goal for the morning: to pick up the radio frequencies from two different swallow-tailed kites he had radioed fourteen months earlier. My job, he said, was to visually locate those same two birds among the thousand or more individuals that would shortly rise up together on the warming air.

"How will I possibly pick them out?" I asked.

"All you have to do is spot the only two birds with transmitter wires extending just beyond their tails—they'll be about the thickness of metal fishing leader, and they shine like silver."

Can't be done, I thought to myself, studying the massed birds staring down at us from the clumped Australian pines, on the verge of simultaneous flight.

"You can do it, I know you can," said Ken, repeating his instructions with complete confidence.

He turned his attention to his receiver, tuning it to the radio frequencies of the young birds. Almost immediately, we heard the steady beeping of first one, then the other, as Ken adjusted the antenna mounted on his white pickup. It was hot on the dike, the air crisp with the rasp of grasshoppers. As Ken went about his work, he described the defining plumage of this year's young birds: shorter tails and fine even-feathered wings. In contrast, the adults bore longer, rattier tails at this time of year, and their flight feathers were uneven as the birds molted old feathers and grew in new.

In twos and threes, then tens and twenties, finally by the hundreds, kites labored off their leafy perches, flapping or diving into the warming air, rounding up into magnificent lifting kettles. I strained my eyes for a silver flash, single-pointed in my resolve to do my very small part.

A colleague, Resee Collins, director of the Audubon Birds of Prey Center, told me recently how she had taken a rehabilitated gunshot kite to Lake Okeechobee, to this same communal premigratory roost, when it was well enough to survive a wild life once again.

"After being able to help so few birds master flight again in this job, it was a thrill to see so many kites flying, in full plum-age, in the wild. Setting that bird free was the right thing to do, the only thing."

She told me how the bird immediately took off with some other kites and how struck she was by the joyful quality of their morning flight.

"They seemed to be fully alive in the present moment; it was like an aerial ballet. There is nothing manmade that could ever compare with that sight. Most amazing of all, in the midst of all these hundreds of soaring birds, the individual I had cared for and released came right by me again, turned on the wing, looked at me. It was like an acknowledgment. Now how do you interpret that? I know I felt connected at that moment.

"No matter how you approach this bird—on a biological, psychological, or sociological level, the common thread is this: they inspire people. That seems to be part of the kite adventure. Even people who don't believe in God, or understand this bird's biological significance, admire them."

"You are lucky," she said to me that day, quietly, as she walked me to my car. "I think they have chosen you to tell their story."

The metallic beeping intensified, snapping me back to the present. Just then, among the many dozens of rapidly rising kites, I glimpsed one with an unmistakable glint of wire against the blue-black of its feathers. Just as miraculously, I spotted the second wired bird.

"Knew you could do it—well done," said Ken.

Flushing in my tiny success, I said, "I'm just going to look down the slope and see if I can find a feather." There was a fence between me and the trees the kites had roosted on, but there, just in front of me, was a flight feather of a swallow-tailed kite, glinting smoky blue on the midday grasses.

I had continued my interviews and conversations with Ken Meyer over the course of several years now, always me interro-

gating, always Ken with the answers, the hypotheses, and whatever certainty there was to be had. And yet even Ken wanted to
know so much more about the swallow-tailed kites' biology. He
was frustrated by how little he still knew of where the birds
went once they left North America. They would simply disap-
pear by mid-September at the very latest and then show up
again in Florida sometime around the first of March.

For all anybody knew the birds were gliding off into noth-
ingness, into the palm of God's hand, or somewhere toward the
long, broad continent to the south.

"In 1992, one of our first field seasons, we only had a few
birds radio-tagged—our methods weren't tight yet, and by the
time several of the radios failed or fell off the birds, we had only
two nestlings with functioning devices," Ken told me.

"One was a young of the year and one was a breeding adult,
both from Bear Island, in the Big Cypress. They disappeared
(as far as we could tell with our tracking gear), and we were real
disappointed. After two weeks we located them in the big Fisheating Creek roost. We monitored them there and got really
good foraging data. The young bird traveled northeast for ten
days, religiously, up to the Brighton Indian reservation; then, all
of sudden, it flew southeast; the adult did the same kind of
thing—reversing its established route and direction. All we
could figure was some premigratory restlessness. My technician
Steve kept checking for their radio signals from the air, finally
locating one bird down near Corkscrew, roosting with several
dozen other kites. Mornings they would head down to Golden
Gates Estates to forage, but what was unusual was that these
birds would return early to the roost, say by one, two, or three
in the afternoon. I took this to mean that they were in migrating
condition and they didn't need to be foraging so much.

"On the fourth of August, Steve and our pilot Karen were
tracking the young bird as usual from the air when he began to
move really fast. My crew had to stop for refueling in Naples.
Steve finally called me and said, 'This bird is really heading out!

I think if we get back up in the air we can follow it. Can I do it? Can we afford the gas and the air time?'

"I said 'Go for it.'

"So up they went, and about 3:30, Steve called again, saying, 'We're still with them, but they're moving toward the coast, down near Cape Romano, and it looks like they're going to move offshore. What should I do?'

"'Stay with them as long as you can, as long as you feel safe going out over the water,' I said. And they did, for another three hours. Eventually they followed that bird about thirteen miles out over the gulf, flying very slowly, southwest. Steve reported how the kite, moving with a small group, would soar up on a thermal to about fifteen hundred feet, then sail off on a southwesterly heading. The birds would gradually lose altitude, but gain mileage, as they coasted off the thermal. Then they'd circle around and find another thermal, beginning the process all over.

"That's how we learned how the kites cross the gulf. At the rate they were going, it probably would take them two days and two nights to get to the tip of the Yucatán Peninsula. My guess is that they'd keep doing that very low energy, efficient kind of flight—even at night. At this time of year, the water temperature out there is in the eighties, warmer than the air, so they keep up that same kind of flight, even in the dark."

We thought for a moment about the kites out there—lifting on invisible thermal swirls, rarely needing to flap a wing, soaring under the ancient stars, repeating their old journeys, rising and moving great distances on the rhythm of heat released from the sea—and we were satisfied.

Still, this was only a small piece of what Ken wanted to know: the "how" part. Even more, he urgently wondered where the kites were going, where they actually spent the winter months. Ken told me he was excited about adding to his toolbox of tracking tools by working with satellite transmitters the next field season, along with the more locally useful radio transmitters I'd seen on his birds this morning. Next season, he hoped actually to follow the kites to their overwintering grounds somewhere in the Southern Hemisphere.

Every bird was far out of our line of sight by now, and the heat of the day had grown fierce. We stowed the tracking gear back in the truck and headed back toward LaBelle, locking the gate to the dike securely behind us. Neither Ken nor I spoke for a time, enjoying the cold conditioned air blowing on our faces from the dashboard vents, pulling deeply on our water bottles. I settled into the passenger seat, flipping through my spiral-bound notebook, rolling up the sleeves of my shirt, wanting to be ready for whatever was to come next.

"I guess you're on your own for a bit," said Ken, unexpectedly, as we pulled into the parking lot where I'd left my car. "I've got to take out some potential funders the next few days." He paused, a bit of apology in his voice. "And I've got this feeling it's time for you to strike out on your own path."

My face burned with rejection, maybe embarrassment, but I didn't disagree. It wasn't really a choice he was offering. Standing in the hot sun, we sorted our gear, untangling our binoculars straps from each other, and my sunscreen and water bottles from his.

"Besides, I'm not sure there's a lot more I can tell you at this point," he said, suddenly all business, focused on the next job on his list. He enfolded me in a quick hug with a promise to keep in touch, and then he was gone.

I was taken off guard. I had blocked out several days more in south Florida, a lifetime, really, thinking to spend it with Ken, assuming I could tag along with whatever fieldwork he had planned, as I had on every visit past. But I couldn't force myself into his expeditions; clearly he believed there wasn't really anything else he could show me. Suddenly I was without a guide.

No keys, either, no helpful technicians, no access to secret nest and roost sites, no radio telemetry data to take me directly to banded kites. No structure. No plan.

I felt all that I didn't know, all my questions, drop deep into my body. And I was afraid.

That night I rented a motel room in Lakeport, the closest place where I could find cheap lodging near the kite roost. I had a disturbing dream.

Somehow I am told that the world will be emptied of all humans because there are too many of us. For some reason, I am given the chance to remain, living in the panhandle of Florida, now devoid of all humanity, as well as any manufactured goods or infrastructure. I am told that I may bring along four other families, as well as my own. Each family will be allotted one large trunk or suitcase, and that's all. My tasks are to quickly decide whom I want to come with us, and then convince them that this situation is real and urgent, and then to pack. I think of who will have the skills to be able to survive with absolutely nothing manufactured: Ann, Gretchen, Donna, and Jody and my stepson Brett. What to pack? I sort through all our drawers and shelves, noting how useless most of our "stuff" is. Should I bring grains and beans? Knives and matches, definitely. A medicine kit? What about David's asthma gear? How can I possibly bring enough of the essentials to last the whole of our remaining lives? I see the impossibility of the task, and I wake, feeling extreme urgency.

I lay in the strange motel bed wondering at the dream and the question it left in its wake. How is it that we name what we truly need? Perhaps only in a survivalist fantasy can we really pare down what is essential to our living, but what about the things that mean more than bare survival, that which must be present if a person, a bird, a community, a planet, is to thrive?

As I pushed out of bed, poured cereal, brewed coffee, I decided that what I really wanted was to see where the kites based at the big premigratory roost might be foraging this late summer morning, how they looked from the ground. Ken had mentioned that some West Palm birders reported seeing kites at a wetland called Lake Hicpochee near Moore Haven. I circled a likely strip of Highway 78 east of Moore Haven on my map and headed out.

A new excitement grew in my belly. I thought of the words of the poet Pablo Neruda: "And something ignited in my soul / fever, or unremembered wings / And I went my own way / deciphering that burning fire."

How do we name what we need, I wondered again, as I drove south. And what it is that we are here to do in our lives on earth?

"To track your own desire, in your own language, is not an isolated task," said the poet Adrienne Rich. I realized that I had been trying to find answers to these questions in the language of my culture, following the paths allowed by the schooling I'd received and according to my parents' hopes and fears and perhaps my grandparents' as well. I began to question that fit.

I thought of Maia, a therapist I'd worked with when I was a graduate student in Gainesville. She tried to help me define what I wanted, my emotional needs. Everything sounded so simple and clear and direct coming out of her mouth. But in order to repeat her words to my partner at home (where I had not been in touch with, nor able to communicate, my real fears, my real needs, or my true desires), I had to speak from the notes I had taken in her office. When I think back to those first few faltering hours, attempting to unravel myself, it reminds me of practicing the skill of walking with a ten-month-old baby. You set the child's small feet on your own, and holding their hands with yours, you step forward, one foot at a time, "Right, left, baby," you say; it's a simple pattern, but when you release your hands, the baby still cannot walk. By myself, even in my mid-twenties, I was having trouble identifying simple truths such as "I am not happy." Or "Something needs to change." Or "We need to talk frankly with each other." It was to be many more years before I could name and speak these things for myself.

Even *to* myself. Many more years before I had the spine to hold fast to my inner voice, no matter the consequence.

Trying to name and decipher what I needed, and what the kites needed, is like straining to identify a bird singing far out in the woods near my porch at home, just at the edge of hearing. It sounds almost like a wood thrush, but I am not always completely sure. Between us is the confounding tangle of sparkleberry and myrtle and oak scrub and the voices of other birds, as well. If the airwaves between me and the thrush were unobstructed, I'd know beyond a doubt its perfect fluting voice, for I have seen it sing. That's how I learned a wood thrush's song, by absorbing its notes with my eyes, my ears, my mind, and my spirit, in an origin-moment of sorts. I was paying attention and able to receive on every possible level, and so I know, and I do not forget.

Maia the therapist tried another tack. She lowered the shades in her office, lit a candle, encouraged me to sit back in my armchair and relax.

"Close your eyes," she said. "Imagine yourself swaddled head to toe in white gauze bandages. Your body is covered with blank white plaster and bandage, just like a mummy. But inside you are alive, the essence of you, all that you are."

I tried to imagine the stiff binding, my body stilled, incubating. I felt claustrophobic but safe in her care.

"Now," she said, "slowly begin to unwrap the shrouding that covers you. Flex your arms, crack the plaster from the inside out, free yourself from this container. Keep unwrapping the bandages." She waited for me to follow her imagery.

"Now tell me, what's inside? What do you see?"

"Nothing, nothing at all," I said, sorrowfully reporting the absolute truth. It wasn't the answer I wanted to give her; I felt like a therapeutic failure.

"I appear to be empty," I repeated, looking into Maia's kind face for guidance, for what to do next. I was astounded with my empty inner "mummy." I wondered what other people would find, given the same exercise. What was I supposed to feel inside? What would it be like to find something other than nothing, when all the structure imposed from without from one's culture was removed? I wanted to build that empty interior into what the counselor/mother/mentor wanted of me, but I also began to see a place to stand that was truly mine: in the absence of me. However insufficient by outer standards, it was mine, I could feel it and know it to be true. A place to truly begin.

Cattle pastures and open savannas gave way to intensive agriculture as I drove toward Moore Haven: citrus, vegetables, sugarcane. The first kite I saw, precisely at the spot Ken predicted, was sharing patrol of an endless field of eight-foot-tall sugarcane with a fat yellow spray plane, both in search of the same insect prey.

What Ken had not predicted was the specter of swallow-tailed kites against the backdrop of Moore Haven itself. Here they were, scores of them, dipping over the Barnett Bank, tilting over Circle K gas. Not high and safely out of reach but hunting singly and low. Low enough to be worshiped. Low enough to be shot.

It was too early to harvest cane; fishing wouldn't pick up until later in the fall. Apparently, in August, no one was in Moore Haven who didn't have to be. The town was a tatter of trailers, broken-down motels, boarded-up bait shops, all pressed tight against Lake Okeechobee's dike by cane fields on three sides. The people seemed poor here, very poor. A heavy young woman slumped on the white metal steps of a rusted double-wide. I steered past two dark-skinned men bent hard over the closed hood of a pickup truck. Right in their midst, kites were clipping through the canopy of the Brazilian pepper hedges, screaming through the yard of a deserted white trailer. No one appeared to notice them at all.

I stopped to watch the kites in a tiny fringe of a park. There were long empty slips painted on the asphalt, room enough for hundreds of trucks and boat trailers. It was clearly a major launching point for anglers at some other time of the year. A shirtless man with a white visor cap was spraying herbicide on the weedy edges of the parking lot and the banks of the canal. His work was so silent, so lethal. The kites continued to swing overhead, so silent, so living.

Heading south out of Moore Haven on Highway 27, I felt agitated and angry. The birds were still all around me; I could spot them thousands of feet up against the mounting cumulus. I saw one so intent on hunting the median of the busy road that it just skipped over the cab of a speeding red pickup. I knew that I didn't want to see the birds here. I wanted them safely back in the preserves and parks, out of sight and reach of 99 percent of the human population. They were too visible here, and they seemed oblivious to their peril. So ancient was their tie to this lake, these once open prairies, this rich mix of flying insects and small vertebrate prey, that they could have no concept of relocating.

There should be worship happening here, I thought, squirming lizards offered on tall prayer sticks, kite likenesses throughout the town. In an earlier time, surely the local peoples noted the return of the kites year after year after year. I could imagine a child running in from a dugout canoe, from the floodplain swamps of Lake Okeechobee, breathless, stumbling, saying, "The kites have arrived! They're here!" The child would be hustled back into the heart of the camp, and all the elders would begin making preparations to mark the return of the kite: prayer ties all over the village, and special rituals, and drumming. There would be those offerings of anole and snake and dragonfly on high poles or platforms around the entrances to the village, all to celebrate the birds and to invite them to bring their energy and their blessings to the native peoples who live in this place where God's birds gather each summer. The wetlands are drying down, and the fish are fat and concentrated in the alligator holes. This is the time of summer fire, the fulcrum between the summer solstice and the fall equinox, a hot, slow time, a time when you might lie on your back and watch the flight of the kites, one of many natural events that allow you to mark time and the passage of the year on your place on the planet. Indigenous peoples must have wondered at the mystery of where the birds go and how was it that these thousands of birds converge on this one place. I imagined that they took the time to reassert the sacredness of this landscape, which calls the swallow-tailed kite to return again and again, and to give thanks for the abundance of the insect and the anole, the things that feed the bird, just as the bird feeds our spirits.

Nothing like that was happening. And I didn't trust the kites to the misery of Moore Haven. I wanted to guard them somehow, but after all, I was the stranger in town. The fact was I didn't trust the kites to myself. My inability to truly protect them stared me in the face.

Lake Okeechobee

The next day, on the broad back of the great dike encircling Lake Okeechobee, I waited, alone. Even at five o'clock in the afternoon, the heat was nearly unbearable. Scanty clouds rose in the west, flowing lakeward, but only a single mushroom-capped thunderhead looked capable of offering rain. And even it appeared unnaturally starved, wavering on its own spindly stalk. Dragonflies surfed the waves of crackling heat built up in the seeding grasses that clung to the dike's sloping shoulder. The odor of melaleuca trees, thick enough to taste—like boiled potatoes with butter, my friend Julie once said—clotted in my mouth. A few vultures scouted the dike just at the height where I hoped I might see a swallow-tailed kite.

Those elusive kites: nowhere in sight. I felt clumsy, leaning against the hood of my blue Datsun station wagon in that empty place. Powerful obstacles lay between us: a dike, a canal, and well-patrolled fences surrounding tens of thousands of acres of very private land. If we were to cross paths, the birds would have to come to me. I might just as well have made an appointment with God as with a wild bird.

But there was this: I knew for a fact that I stood within a scant mile or two of thousands of swallow-tailed kites. I had chosen this watch post carefully, hoping to maximize the chances of encountering them when they began to return to their nightly resting spot.

It wasn't as uncertain an enterprise as it would have been ten years earlier. Since 1929, sixty years before Ken Meyer began his studies of swallow-tailed kites in Florida, concentrations of these birds, apparently migrating, had been reported in the summer months along the south and west shores of Lake Okeechobee. Yet the existence of the communal night roost I visited with Ken was not discovered until 1987. It is a tribute to the remoteness of the enormous acreage of private ranchlands in this part of Florida that such a phenomenon could go unmarked for so long. State wildlife biologist Brian Millsap was the one who finally pinpointed the kite roost. In the summer of 1986, working a hunch, using all the tools and training at his disposal—deep curiosity, extensive familiarity with raptors, and the scientific literature—and persistence, he repeatedly drove the public roads immediately south and west of the lake.

Late on the morning of July 26, Millsap hit pay dirt: twenty-five kites moving southeast in twos and threes on a steady flight line. Millsap prowled State Road 78 in his green Commission vehicle, back and forth, back and forth, eventually spotting soaring flocks of one hundred to two hundred birds that coalesced and moved to the northwest. Millsap haunted the area, returning half a dozen days, seeking flight patterns that would shed light on what the kites might be doing. He noted that the late afternoon movements of the birds were the reverse of the expected southward orientation of migrants in south Florida. Although he could not verify his suspicion that first summer, the next summer Millsap arranged a flyover, and the sight that greeted him was worth the wait: nearly a thousand swallow-tailed kites crowded into the tops of a stand of cypress trees, surrounded by a deep, thickly vegetated freshwater marsh. Several days later he tallied more than thirteen hundred birds leaving the roost. Over the next two weeks he watched the numbers shrink dramatically, in synchrony with their suspected migration to the Southern Hemisphere.

A friend once asked me, "If they're so hard to find, why are you so obsessed with swallow-tailed kites? Why didn't you choose something closer to home, like a cardinal, or a Carolina wren?" It's true: if I had chosen the purple gallinule or the bald eagle, the marsh hawk or the ever-present alligator, this would be a simpler story to tell. If I had selected one of those, I could have pages of notes, hours and hours of dependable observations from a single locale near my home. I love so many birds; why hanker after the one so seldom seen?

What if I were to see a kite at this moment, if that wing-spread gull coming off the lake were the bird I seek, what would be different? My reaction to kites is physical, so my skin would prickle, adrenalin would pump into my bloodstream, and my mind would snap into focus. I would track the bird intently for the brief time it was in my sight. Later, I would turn those minutes over and over in my mind, like a first embrace with a long-anticipated lover: What was it doing? Where might it have been headed, and to do what?

Unlike me, the marsh fringing the lake below me appears choiceless. It supports the ibis and the little blue heron equally, wherever their weight can be borne. The presence or absence of seasonal creatures doesn't seem to affect its basic nature.

But that "why?" is worth asking, no matter what the content of one's obsession. No one is paying me to study kites or to write about them, and unlike Meyer or Millsap, I'm not going to make a big contribution to science. No one really cares if I follow kites at all.

Still, the swallow-tail has me completely. I belong to it. The bird is woven into my tendons; it is the part of me that can fly, that goes directly into the mystery. It is that within me that longs to drift over river bottoms, that is strong and light and swift, both vulnerable and eternal, that stays where it belongs no matter what has happened to that place until there is no way to live there anymore.

I'm beginning to think my preoccupation with this bird has everything to do with the longing it sets in motion in my own spirit. I think back to Brian Millsap, how he discovered the awesome, miraculously overlooked kite roost, how he had to piece together anecdote and clue and intuition before he brought in the big guns of science and airplane to confirm his discovery. I think my attraction to kites is not so serendipitous after all. How little was known of these birds until so recently. How little we know of the roots of our longing, how we take more than we need to fill up our empty spaces.

A crested caracara, little-known Florida specialty, breaks my reverie, twisting free of the air and dropping to the edge of the road below me. Smaller than a vulture, larger than a crow, it highsteps on thick yolk-yellow legs to the water at the base of a boat ramp. It pants through its thick red bill. I can relate. I didn't expect to need so much drinking water this late in the day, and I'm mostly standing still. A single swallow-tail, apparently flushed by an airboat buzzing in the hidden canal beyond the dike, swings close. It hunts the line of melaleuca trees ringing the marsh, inspecting closely the outermost branchlets, then glides to the road and begins a tightly spiraled float straight up and out of sight.

Across the road, the caracara hops onto a low fence post, then picks its way down the blacktop, foraging on small dead carrion. Its step brightens, quickens when cars approach, and it brushes ten or twenty feet off the road through a thigh-high sway of flowering bahia grass.

Farther in the distance, in a young sweet gum tree, I catch a glimpse of a red-bellied woodpecker working its way along a rotten limb. The bird beats into the fist of the snag, following its hunger through dead wood to insect. For these birds, no difference between want or desire and true need. How did we humans come to be so complicated, so confused between our wants and our needs?

Birds don't seem at all plagued by the restless dreams and moody despairs that sometimes taunt me. It may be just these yearnings, born in the limbic portion of my three-in-one human brain, that set me apart from birds and other animals. Our limbic brains—sandwiched between the reptilian brain we share with birds and the neocortex, which allows us to reason—house the desires that distinguish us and the abilities we develop to play and to nurture and to interact socially. In contrast, birds take their cues to choose a mate, nest, and migrate from external factors such as day length and prey abundance. Physical closeness between birds has to do with optimizing resources. It's pragmatic, not linked and loaded, as it is for humans, with desire and loneliness. When there is sexual connection, it is correlated with reproduction, and there seems to be a comfort with separation of bodies, a greater pause between moments of physical closeness.

I continue to watch the caracara between binocular sweeps for kites; often all I can see is its brown back, bent over the refuse of the road. It flies to the top of a vine-covered cabbage palm, takes up some kind of watch. The only thing that makes caracaras subtle, I decide, is how preoccupied we are, how quickly we drive through the places they live. Eventually dark comes, but no cool air and no more kites.

The next afternoon, I once again resumed my post on the Okeechobee dike. It was a very different day. Long drifts of gray rain in the west promised little chance of clearing—or swallow-tails. My brain strained to convert the tiny black floaters in my eyes into kites, but they simply weren't there. I fretted and paced the narrow trail and finally decided to drive south to Moore Haven and around to Palmdale, casting about for encounter. As I drove, I tried to chide myself out of the inexplicably strong longing that keeps me returning to this time and place, this bird. Then I remembered a time, several months ago, when I heard that the next morning between 3 and 6 a.m. would be the closest full moon—that full moon within the calendar year when the moon is nearest to our planet. I set the alarm for 5:00 a.m. so I could walk toward that moon, hoping for something, wanting at least to be bathed in the light of it, facing it, it facing me, nothing between us except 226,000 miles of space, the least there ever would be this year.

When I stepped out my front door into the cool young day, the shadow of the house on the sharp grass stood stark, an over-exposed negative. Tall pines sieved the moonlight into long shards over the garden and field. I could sense the dryness of the road and the thin veil of red clay dust I stirred with my shoes. The moon globe, three-dimensional in its fullness, lit my path to the west. I wanted no intervention between me and all that the rare light could infuse.

Walking toward that closest full moon was so like chasing kites. They are both unreachable; you can never really get there, not on their own wild terms. But you can look after something holy, and I wonder if just having mind and spirit and body so oriented, to the simple moon or a particular bird, isn't somehow for the greater good.

Driving on in the rain, I turned in the traffic heading toward Palmdale and finally spotted a kite, then ten others, perched in an enormous dead melaleuca tree. Exactly where I had seen them a year before. I pulled into the center turn lane, pointed my car straight toward them. They were preening, perched like so many blackbirds in the candelabra of the tree. I debated whether to park on this busy road, determined to out-wait the weather here as long as they did. My engine was still running when, one by one, the birds dropped from the tree and flapped directly over my car. I leaned out the window into the rain, looked straight up into their dark eyes, their white bellies, their molting wings. "Beautifuls, beautifuls, where are you going?" I called. They tilted on regardless, not hunting but heading homeward, across fields of raspy sugarcane toward the roost, miles to the north. Even as I worshiped the birds, they continued unmoved on their necessary journeys. As they passed over me, salt tears of thankfulness and yearning mingled in my eyes, and I felt closer to obsession, and paradoxically to a state of grace, than I ever had before.

The poet Linda Hogan has written, "Many of us in this time have lost the inner substance of our lives and have forgotten to give praise and remember the sacredness of all life. But in spite of this forgetting, there is still a part of us that is deep and intimate with the world. . . . We experience it as a murmur in the night, a longing and restlessness we can't name, a yearning that tugs at us. . . . Something in our human blood is still searching for [the ancient connections between people and land], still listening, still remembering."

I think about her words, wonder if the way I've allowed my longing to coalesce around kites is too much to ask of them in these times and too little to ask of myself. Clearly, I can't go where these kites are going. That's not why I'm here. Nor am I here to study them, at least not as these scientists are. My work seems to be to investigate, to experience them, on a very different level. They force me to study my longing, our collective longings, which I believe at core are for intimacy. These hungers didn't begin with us. We merely play out their urgencies, as if we hung on to the end of a long line of ice-skaters, clutching the next hand in line, moving swiftly over the ice, cracking the whip: and we are that tail, pulled by others before us, and our accumulated desires, and in our attempt to compensate for what has been lost, we overcompensate and careen out of control, hurting not only ourselves but all of the planet.

Like Shooting at the Moon

On a dark morning in May, I picked along a rain-shiny
boardwalk at Blue Spring State Park. I had just finished a pre-
sentation to a group of park biologists, and my arms were still
crammed with the stuff of bureaucracy: oversized maps, a
floppy briefcase overflowing with speech notes and papers. Even
though I'd made good professional connections, I felt bruised
by a long drive through hail the night before and hard times at
home. Cold droplets pecked against all the green leaves and slid
behind my glasses. I couldn't tell if it was I or the sky that was
crying, nor exactly why. My chest felt full, swollen to the point
of breaking. Driving south from Tallahassee to Deland the
evening before, I had seen only one kite, just north of Perry, but
it didn't satisfy, wheeling high and away from me, indifferent,
unattainable. Huge black clouds coalesced into an ominous
thunderstorm that seemed to swallow everything south of Orange Lake, and I had to slow my truck to twenty-five miles per
hour. Hail beat on the metal roof; the truck's wipers swiped ice
fragments off and into the streaming bed of the interstate.

The unexpected sight of a swallow-tailed kite coasting over
the spring run grasped me by the heart and shook me a bit from
my despair. The bird soared just above the restored forest, over
cabbage palms that snaked across the jewel blue water, shaking
their long shredded leaves into the midspaces of the oak canopy.
The bird seemed to smooth the air above the azure water with
subtle continuous movements of wing and tail, molding the
invisible aura of the place into alignment. Its work, the work of
angels. How I longed for that peaceful duty, riding the crystal
breath of the spring and the exhale of the trees, coaxing the
forest into something else, something more, something I could
not name, except by its absence in myself.

☙

I continued south, winding my way around Lake Sybelia, through what seemed likely to be the only green space remaining in urban Orlando, to visit the birds-of-prey rehabilitation center run by the Florida Audubon Society. Here, I'd learned, three swallow-tailed kites resided in the permanent custody of curator Resee Collins and her staff. I smiled to myself, thinking that this may be the only stop on my journey after kites where I can make an appointment to see them and they must honor it.

As I entered the leafy, fenced facility, I ran my eyes quickly over the exhibited birds: kestrels, two screech owls, a barn owl, a merlin. But where were the swallow-tails?

Resee Collins, the curator of the Audubon Center for Birds of Prey, strode out to meet me; she had just returned from one of the hundreds of educational programs she presents each year.

"If I hadn't been giving a formal talk, you'd never catch me in these white pants," she laughed, shaking my hand. She led me to a small rectangular yard, almost a garden, and there was the bird I sought, the bird as I'd never seen one before: thoroughly grounded. The kite hunched on a low wire perch, tethered by a rope about two feet long.

Resee told me that the bird was a gunshot victim, permanently crippled by a fractured radius of the right wing. This kite, shot right out of the blue Florida sky, will never fly again. Never feel the tightening of air against muscle nor direct its powerful, complicated eyes after any prey beyond the circumference of its short tether. Resee invited me closer, but the bird didn't recognize me and panicked, fluttering in the opposite direction, to the grassy lawn, to the end of its rope. I hastily retreated to a distance that allowed the bird to relax and settled my own body into an awkward crouch. I felt a strong sense of the potential to force a relationship with this captive bird. Neither of us wanted that.

Resee handed me a bucket of mealworms caked in peaty soil

and showed me how to offer them to the tethered kite. It took the wriggling food as fast as I could clean the small, glistening creatures of soil, tens of them, maybe a hundred. It was a painstaking process, and the bird showed no indication of getting full. The kite was beautiful, but I noticed that its tail was broken and awkward.

Resee knelt closer to the kite, her brown ponytail swinging against her back. The skin around her eyes crinkled with affection. She explained that it is hard to keep swallow-tails fully feathered in captivity, since they are often in permanent tail molt.

"It's because of the shape of their bodies," she said. "I would describe them as Rubenesque: they're very stocky, with short, thick legs and tails almost two times the length of their bodies. They keep molting in new tail feathers and breaking them."

Outside the nesting season during daylight hours, swallow-tailed kites are nearly always airborne. These most aerial of birds rarely land in trees, except to roost at night, and they never light on the ground or in water. Kites have never been reported in the scientific literature walking, climbing, or hopping. And they select roost trees so tall that their tails could grow meters long without touching the ground. I thought of the birds high on a thermal updraft or drinking while skimming Lake Hicpochee or the cold clear boil of Wakulla Springs, all the ways I have seen them—but never like this.

Resee didn't focus on this kite's physical limitations. She pointed out the exquisite tracery of dark veins on the white feathers of its head and the blue "window" patch on its wing.

"The Seminoles called this the window to the Creator," she said, feeding the bird with the surety of long acquaintance and experience. "Through this window, it is said, the Creator views our world, and so these birds are thought to be messengers between the world above and the world below."

Excited by our conversation, I accidentally knocked over the plastic container of mealworms. They were too expensive to leave in the grass, uneaten, and the kite wouldn't be able to pick them all up before they burrowed into the dirt, so we sorted them slowly from the grass blades and soil and fed them alternately to the kite and a one-eyed burrowing owl tethered nearby.

"Let me introduce you to our other two kites," said Resee, leading me through a narrow passageway between two covered sets of airy cages, each about five by ten feet, outfitted with wooden perches and blue plastic watering troughs. Two kites were housed in the first cage on the left. Resee pointed out that one had orange eyes, the other black. I'd never been close enough before to notice. Both colors occur naturally in wild kites, she said.

One of these birds was found inexplicably emaciated in Volusia County; the other, shot, somewhere in central Florida. Resee clipped a short lead onto the foot of the orange-eyed bird. He settled quickly onto the heavy, elbow-length glove Resee had donned and ruffled his feathers so that he appeared twice his normal size.

"That's called rousing," Resee smiled. "The bird exerts the muscles in its skin and shakes its feathers up. Young birds do it a lot." What privilege to know these birds, or any animal for that matter, well enough to recognize and name their behaviors.

Resee talked about how the kites clearly take comfort in one another's company and how their sociality extends even to their human caretakers.

"They will call to you when you come out in the morning or when you go into the mouse house. They're definitely laid back, more gregarious and social and gentle than most of the other raptors."

Resee read the longing in my eyes. She slipped the bulky falconer's glove onto my arm, then handed me the bird. My eyes filled with gratitude for the chance to be so close, but the kite floundered, straining away, panting, and again I had a sense of forcing relationship. The agitated animal suddenly defecated, spraying an arcing pattern of feces on me, Resee, the cage. Clumsily, I handed the bird back. Even though I believed my intentions were good, I was asking for an intimacy I had not earned.

In the early days of ornithology, it was common practice to shoot a great quantity of wild birds to identify, study, and preserve. Museum skin collections offer scientific documentation and allow close examination of birds whose identity might be otherwise difficult or impossible to determine. Nineteenth-century bird students, including John James Audubon and Frank M. Chapman, had no apparent difficulty merging their admiration of a bird with its murder.

"As I neared the lake, there came floating over one of the most beautiful birds I ever saw, a Swallow-tailed Kite," wrote Frank Chapman in his *Journals*, published in 1887. "Three times I fired without effect. It was like shooting at the moon."

And consider the words of turn-of-the-century scientist Albert Franklyn Ganier, a student of Mississippi kites. After observing a family of fledgling kites in their nest for several days, Ganier wrote: "[My] affection for [the young bird] grew so strong that my gun was commissioned to add his skin to my collection." There is very little difference between Ganier's passion and an even stronger desire to fully possess the object of his affections.

What do we know, after all, about encouraging passion and teaching limits? About possession?

It was only in the mid-twentieth century that Roger Tory Peterson led the science of bird study away from gunning, assisted by the advance of binoculars and spotting scopes.

"I consider myself to have been the bridge between the shotgun and the binoculars in birdwatching," Peterson was quoted in a newspaper wire story just before his death in 1996. "Before I came along, the primary way to observe birds was to shoot them and stuff them."

Most raptors, including hawks, owls, and kites, have suffered far more under the guns of common folk than ornithologists. Swallow-tailed kites, exceedingly vulnerable as a result of their tame and curious natures, were (and probably still are) shot through idle "plinking" by scattered individuals giving no particular thought beyond cause (shooting a gun) and effect (hitting an enticing target).

In the 1958 edition of *Georgia Birds,* edited by Thomas Burleigh, the entry for swallow-tails states: "It is unfortunate that the indiscriminate shooting of all hawks in Georgia has so reduced the numbers of the Swallow-tailed Kite that it is now a scarce bird everywhere in the state. Attractive in appearance and entirely beneficial in its food habits, it deserved protection at all times, and its present scarcity is a sad commentary on the general attitude towards our birds of prey."

Modern-day ornithologists Dr. Bill Robertson and John Cely believe there is a direct correlation between the kite's elimination from its range in the Mississippi drainage north to Wisconsin and the movement of European settlers across the midwestern landscape of North America. Robertson suggests that swallow-tails were especially vulnerable to shooting because of their unwariness around humans; the fact that they were "attractive" targets; and because most settlers were equipped with guns.

Of the twelve swallow-tailed kites admitted to the Madeleine Baldwin Birds of Prey Center since 1981, eight were gunshot victims. And of those, only two have been rehabilitated and released.

During this time I had a dream: *There is a local kite that people in the area all know. But a woman living alone deep in the woods shot it because she feared it, even though she said all she had*

seen it do was capture moths from a perch under her elevated cabin.
She couldn't take a chance, she said, she couldn't afford its wildness.
Then we heard about another kite shot. I had pushed away this form
of threat, and now I have to worry about it again. Individual people
do shoot kites. It's not just anonymous growth and development that
threatens the kites. You can't assume people won't shoot, I dreamed.

Kites, as well as eagles, hawks, and other raptors, received no legal protection from persons in possession of a gun
and ill intent until very recently. In 1918, the Migratory Bird
Treaty Act and its implementation in the United States marked
the end of two exploitative practices decimating several other
groups of wild birds: spring hunting of waterfowl, and the
shooting of herons and egrets for their breeding plumes. Hawks
and their allies were not covered by the act and remained
subject to uncontrolled killing until 1972, when the act was
amended to grant them full federal protection from indiscriminate shooting.

Even as legislated protection has increased, there has been
an escalating rash of violence directed against all undefended
beings in our culture, not just birds of prey. I know manatee
activists, and even a legislator, who have emerged from county
commission meetings to be doused by bleach thrown on their
clothing and to find slashed tires on their cars. There are women
speaking out in public forums on behalf of the heavily polluted
Fenholloway River in Perry, Florida, who have been raped and
beaten for refusing to be silenced. What is the root of all this
violence, anger, and will to power? What fear lies behind these
actions and emotions? How deep is this fear that soft bodies
stand in its path? How wounded is it that it must wound? I do
not think we are done yet with the shooting of kites, no matter
the good intent of our laws.

Put Your Body over the Precious Things

The only daylight interval when a swallow-tailed kite in the wild remains still enough to be observed is when she is nesting. In Big Cypress National Preserve, the month of April is that time. Ken offered to set me up for a night and two days near a nest tree he'd found; he had his technician deliver me and my camping gear—heavy black duffel, tent, gallon water bottle, and day pack—alongside the Eleven-mile Road deep in the preserve. I hauled my gear a quarter of a mile east, within shouting distance of the swallow-tail pair, and quickly pitched my tent. I stowed a simple supper of crackers and cheese and raw vegetables in my pack and circled the nest tree, looking for a vantage site. The sun burned warm and bright, even in late afternoon.

I selected a skinny, fallen cypress trunk to settle on; my perch faced north toward the unusually bifurcated slash pine where the kite incubated her eggs. As I backed into place, a second kite—her mate?—materialized and called insistently over me. Then he vanished, and I saw him only one more time that evening, floating high, high above.

Two hours later, the nest-bound kite had yet to move. Her snowy head, brilliantly lit by the setting sun, must surely help her mate locate her from the high clouds, I thought. No sign of other kites. The nest tree rocked in the light breeze. The bird remained still. That was her work. I, on the other hand, shifting my weight on the hard log, was not as clear about exactly what I was doing there. And as evening approached, doubt rose—and fear.

I wanted very much to be there, alone, but the female swallow-tailed kite, with only her long black tail and pearly head visible, didn't seem to be doing a thing. Except this:

through my binoculars, I could see that she was staring at me. Just above her, a six-inch pinecone hung in the bundling emerald needles. Two noisy flycatchers moved restlessly from snag to pine to cypress, although they never landed on the kite's pine. Longing for something to happen, I munched on purple cabbage and watched her back, a living incubator of hidden life, the next turn.

By dusk, at 7:30, there was nothing more to see of the Big Cypress National Preserve. And it was very quiet, only one chuck-will's-widow calling for company. I was bedded down in my sleeping bag with all the fears my active mind could conjure and ready to bargain with the universe for what seemed like my life.

Only allow me to see my son to eighteen, to adulthood, I prayed. Only allow me more time to become more compassionate, of more use to this planet. Only let me return home, this one time. Only let me live with awareness, attention, joy. What is it that I was really asking? Only let me be safe.

The chuck fell quiet. A heron croaked. Cryptic insects blurred the edges of utter silence with mild white noise. Far away an airboat or airplane sounded. A second chuck picked up far to the west. It was very dark. I could almost imagine through my tent, squarely pitched between the east and the west, that I could see the horizon glow of Naples and Miami. Did the kite, in her nest, feel them pressing? Did she sense the fragile interlude that separated us, her and me, from the cities and men with guns?

If I had a gun, I might relax, I thought.

If I were strong and trained in karate.

But even having burly male companions hadn't always dampened my fear when it came rising.

I noticed how my whole body was in love with living and how my mind bargained against the night fears, yearned for morning. I fingered my pocketknife—slim protection. I rehearsed the emergency radio directions and tried to figure how deep terror must run before it overrides pride, forcing me to send out a plea by radio airwave for rescue. I considered building a fire, sitting up all night awake, standing guard against fear with flame. I wondered which was the crazy part of me that thought up this idea and weighed the time away from life with family, from work and responsibility and garden and home, against my desire to be with the kites.

Crested flycatchers and a wild turkey gobbling woke me before six. It took the sun a long time to burn off the gentle settle of damp fog that silenced the woods during the night. As the sun pierced through, I delighted in the ground cover around me: sawgrass, wiregrass, dozens of sedges and rushes and herbs, shining with fine beads of dew.

From my post on the cypress log, I hadn't been able to see the female kite through the fog. At seven, the male appeared and circled the tree three times, flapping and gliding, just at canopy level, soundless. The female dove off the nest and disappeared to the west. The male perched at the edge of the nest for just seconds, then gradually settled down facing the sherbet-orange sunrise.

While the kite sat tight, the singers of the subtropical pinewoods—meadowlarks, bluebirds, Carolina wrens, nuthatches, gnatcatchers, and a whole suite of woodpeckers—had their say. The sounds were nearly the same as home, 450 miles to the north.

At home, I long for these wild places; at home, kites pass over very rarely. But at home, my job is mostly tending my child, and I'm grateful for the years I've had, his first five, to care for him myself. I think of containing his conceived body inside mine and birthing him and the uncounted times I have held the length of his small body against mine. This body of my child I will do anything to protect. Like the kite on her eggs. When I am not home with him, even though I know he is well,

I miss him, and I cannot tell if this work following kites justifies my absence from his days.

About every ninety minutes, the parent kites exchanged places on the nest. A typical interaction looked like this: at 8:25, a single bird approached from the northwest, circled the tree three times, called *wheet-wheet-wheet* two or three times, then landed on the crown of the tree, several yards from the nest. The second bird immediately took off, heading southwest. The first bird snugged down over the unseen eggs. At 8:30, five minutes later, the second bird returned, circled the vicinity of the nest silently, then headed out again. You could easily miss the whole thing if you turned your head for just the barest moment.

It was getting very hot in the sun; my energy ebbed. Scores of white ibis winged overhead, dividing their group to skirt me. As I watched the unmoving kite parents, it was hard to imagine how my nest vigil could help with the conservation tasks at hand.

Be still for now, the white head of the swallow-tailed kite appeared to say. *Protect what is life affirming, life beginning, without rancor. Hold fast to what is right. Speak truthfully. And place your body over the precious things.*

At noon, the radio signaled—my ride out of the swamp had arrived. It was time to leave the kites to their eggs. As I gathered my gear, I realized they didn't need my help here: they offered their unborn the only protection required—their own warm bodies. What I had to do was to go back into my life and see to their protection in other ways.

Edge of the Range

Later in the summer, I traveled to Pearl River, Louisiana, with favorite companions: my oldest friend, Elise, and her son, Matt. With a highly respectable birding "life list" of 565 species, fourteen-year-old Matthew was particularly interested in this trip: although he had birded all over the world traveling with his family, he had yet to see a swallow-tailed kite.

Matt thumbed through his bird books as we drove, passing the spread-open guides to the front seat so his mother could study the bird we hoped to see today.

Elise, an art historian, marveled at the strength of contrast between black and white on the swallow-tail.

"How, when you're talking about such little feathers, can the lines be so sharply drawn between dark and light on this bird's body?" she wondered. "Maybe some of its power, what draws us, is created by that tension. Nothing can be further apart coloristically than all colors—black; and no color—white." She explained how, from an artist's point of view, color can be a distraction, can actually take away from the power of the artist's message and dilute the intended emotional impact.

I remembered a pamphlet I read after my son's birth, about how newborn infants are more attracted to high-contrast black-and-white patterns than they are to color or brightness. Toy stores now offer a whole line of mobiles, toys, and cards for babies based on the earliest visual preferences of humans for bold black-and-white images.

"Maybe this early attraction adds weight to our later attraction to certain animals: black panthers, white ibis, polar bears, pandas, wood storks—and swallow-tailed kites," I suggested.

Matthew said: "It seems like there's so much happening with these kites that builds up this feeling of contrast we get from the bird's plumage, like how precise and punctual they are in their nesting dates and yet how unpredictable they can be to actually see. Like now, I'd really like to see one!"

It was easy to pick out our guides, Jennifer and Tom Colson, at a boat ramp on the West Pearl River near Exit 5a of Interstate 59—the border between Louisiana and Mississippi. Jennifer, in pink-flowered shorts and a sleeveless taupe shirt, had a bulky headset clamped over her ears and her silky, waist-length brown hair. Tom hovered close by, almost protectively, holding an antenna high while Jennifer carefully scanned her receiver for the separate frequencies of the three juvenile kites she had outfitted with transmitting radios just weeks before.

The couple nodded a cordial hello as we got out of the car but didn't converse until each young kite was accounted for. Fast-moving traffic clacked rhythmically over the interstate bridge, and the hot July sun rose through the trees directly into our faces. Matt scanned those trees for kites—any birds, really. Mississippi kite, he pointed. Great crested flycatcher. Fish crow. Red-bellied woodpecker. Broad-winged hawk, in heavy molt.

"Hey, we got all three signals. I'm happy!" Jennifer finally called over to us, relaxing with a squinty-eyed smile. She freed her long earrings from the headphones and her hair. Tom disassembled their gear.

"But you probably won't see them—they're hanging deep in that swamp."

With a wave, she indicated the river and the trees beyond: from here this swamp extended for miles, and access to its interior was next to impossible.

Jennifer Colson, a falconer and biology instructor in her mid-twenties, lived in Arabi, Louisiana, about fifteen miles east of New Orleans. She was among the four or five scientists from as many agencies who had begun to explore the status of swallow-tailed kites at the western edge of their range—that uncertain edge between extinction and embodiment—in southern Mississippi and Louisiana and extreme southeastern Texas. Her primary aim was to locate premigration roosts of kites for two reasons: first, all the birds spotted so far during migration in her part of the country were heading due west, not south toward the Lake Okeechobee congregation in Florida; and second, she figured that finding groups of birds in roosts would be easier than looking for single, "dinner plate–sized" nests one hundred feet up in pine trees.

With Ken Meyer's advice and technical support (he sent her several transmitters to place on Gulf Coast birds), Jennifer managed to radio-tag three juvenile kites during the 1995 breeding season. From what she told me over the telephone, working with these "suburban kites" was quite different from the nesting situations I'd observed on public lands in Florida.

And in fact, Jennifer was able to locate and work with them with remarkable ease, unlike Ken Meyer's excruciating searches in Florida. To illustrate, the Colsons led us to one of her study sites in the nearby town of Pearl River, the home of Jean and John Wilson.

As we pulled into the drive, Elise and I agreed that the low brick home, settled under old pines and draped in pink-flowering mandevilla vines, could be straight off the pages of *Southern Living* magazine. Jennifer walked us around back to the multilayered outdoor deck. Over these potted perennials, above these very water gardens and feeders and reclining chairs, Jennifer told us, two young kites were successfully reared and fledged just weeks ago. It was a real stretch to imagine nineteen adult swallow-tailed kites roosting here, as they did from March until early July—the setting seemed far too domesticated for the elusive bird I'd studied.

Jean Wilson, a gracious blonde woman in her mid-fifties, came out the back door of her home to greet us and tell her story.

"The kites actually have nested here for two years, although we'd seen them around for all of the six years we've lived in this house," said Jean. "I didn't know a thing about them, but

they were so unusual that I began to wonder if they were endangered or something. I called around for advice, and someone
gave me Jennifer's name." The two women became good
friends, compatriots in the cause of kites.

"I work in the yard a lot," Wilson said. "I got so I knew the
parents' delivery call, and I would look to see what they were
bringing the young birds for dinner. I thought they were really
good parents; often two birds would accompany the one with
the food when it fed the babies."

Jean Wilson saw that lots of wasp nests with fat larvae inside
were among the babies' first foods ("sometimes the parents
brought in wasp nests still attached to a tree branch!"). As the
chicks grew, the adult birds delivered other kinds of insects and
many snakes to their young. Jean and Jennifer collected the
discarded, indigestible "castings" that tumbled from the nest to
sort and identify. Once the women saw a live female red bat
come flopping out of the nest after the intended food item
slipped from the grip of an unpracticed baby kite. Jean's husband erected a beach umbrella over their barbecue grill to protect it from the cementlike droppings the kites ejected over the
side of the nearly convex nest.

Jennifer and Jean told us that these "suburban" kites
were extremely tolerant of people, even when Jennifer rented a
massive crane to lift her to the nest so she could band and radio-
tag the young birds.

"We were so nervous," said Jennifer. "The crane took forever, knocking branches off some of the surrounding trees. It
even got stuck for half an hour. But we had to make it work
because it was our only chance to tag the young, and at four
hundred dollars a pop, it wasn't like we could rent the crane
twice!

"With all that obnoxious machinery and two people working
with the young chicks, the female still delivered food while we
were up there."

Jean said: "Even on the fourth of July, with firecrackers popping throughout the neighborhood, the kites stayed put. Based on our experience, I've come to the conclusion that they actually like people!"

Some of the most poignant observations the women made were of reluctant, would-be fledglings. The adults were very attentive, always escorting the young in pairs, threesomes, or more as they learned to fly and ventured from the nest. The adults used trickery to encourage their babies' independence. Jean watched a begging, long-fledged youngster frustrated into its own foraging for food; its caretakers would deliver it only big bunches of inedible lichens. And when another fledgling kept returning to its natal tree instead of flying, the adults blocked it, actually bumping the chick, forcing it to stay airborne and away.

Before this property was fashioned into comfortable suburban living quarters, it was simply the high ground just upwater of the Morgan River Swamp, one of the widespread wetlands of the Pearl River. The river itself meanders one-half mile to the east; here a built-up levee protects the property of the Wilsons and their neighbors from flood. To a kite's eye, from the air, then, this habitat is identical in structure to the nesting choices of Florida kites: the tallest pine or two on high ground adjacent to a swamp teeming with suitable prey—arboreal snakes and frogs and satisfactory insect populations. It is just that people now build houses right under those tallest of pines, right up to the edge of the swamp.

Before we left Pearl River, Jennifer showed us the other two nest trees she'd worked this breeding season, both in the heart of similarly wooded residential communities. An obvious concern seemed to me that not all homeowners might consider the kites a blessing or a privilege, something very special to be protected. Jennifer agreed and told us that when one of these young birds took its first flight, unsteadily circling a busy municipal swimming pool full of kids, it was greeted with noisy screams and thrown water toys. And the land the Wilsons' kites nest on actually adjoined theirs: Century 21 has posted a "For Sale" sign and a $72,000 price tag.

"I'm really concerned about the swallow-tailed kites, that something might go wrong for them," said Jennifer, explaining why she permitted her busy life to be stretched ever thinner, studying kites. So far, she had received support from the National Biological Survey to purchase equipment for her nesting study, and from Ken Meyer, but no salary from anywhere. It was simply a labor of love.

"Our work this year all came together at the last moment. Next season, I'm going to try and radio-tag five or six birds. Somehow I'll make it happen," she continued, reflecting. "I'll do it because it needs to be done."

In the car heading north to Jackson, we talked about Jennifer, about Jean Wilson, about how and why people respond to birds, about what form that affection can take. In the back seat, I finally spotted a swallow-tailed kite, our one and only for the day. The bird dipped improbably low over the highway, and Matthew drank in the terrific, terribly brief interval it remained in our sight.

"This is the best bird on my list since Jerusalem—the hoopoe. Or maybe the trogon at Ramsey Canyon," said my nephew, reflectively. "I can see how it might come to obsess you."

It didn't seem like a good time to tell Matthew how precarious this kite's future seemed to me.

Death of Birth

I wanted to visit a place where kites had been extirpated, where their ancient territories had been so altered that
these birds could no longer recognize or use them as range. I
wanted to explore what it might feel like to be in such a landscape, sponged clear of its wildness, its kites.

One way it feels is like unnatural, thigh-deep mud. One way
it smells is like deadened backwater.

My friends and I crossed an old local bridge linking the state
of Mississippi with the west, searching for access to the river's
edge. It wasn't easy to find. Behind a great levee at aptly named
Delta, Louisiana, we parked at a boat ramp and began to race
the children across the bank to touch the swift water. Yards
from the river, startled and laughing, we sank to our knees, then
our thighs, in backed-up Mississippi mud. This, we realized, was
rich residue the river had intended to distribute over miles of
floodplain, now unnaturally contained behind broad levees. It
could neither dry nor spread itself, as the river desired.

Immobilized to midthigh by the warm mire, I arched back,
easily defying balance, searched the sky to see what might fly
here. Some early swallows dipped across the empty volumes of
air; farther upriver, I saw turkey vultures tilting. But nowhere to
the north, nor for many miles south, might the drifting profile
of a swallow-tail still be glimpsed. The engineering of our own
species had erased that possibility quite thoroughly.

I understood the magnitude of the landscape loss in the
continent's largest river floodplain even better when I flew over
the Mississippi on my way to Montana. Sixty-seven miles north
of Memphis, the pilot pointed out the river, thirty-five thousand
feet directly below. From that height, the broad channel seemed
a frozen mirror, without motion, leashed and shackled by cir-
clets of dike and dam and diversion canal.

At one time, the Mississippi played among a thousand sparkling backwaters and bars. There was all the time and space the broad river required to create and nourish its great floodplain forests with silty sustenance. Now, only a flat tracery on the surface of the land remained of the fertile crescent oxbows that had twined about the muddy mother-channel, their shadows now etched into fields of row crops like those of human bodies into concrete at Hiroshima. That much of death have we inflicted on our continent's mightiest river, so truncated now, so carefully engineered. There is no allowance for surprise or whimsy, except in the occasional destructive fury of a swollen spring, when the river, like a desperate prisoner, makes a break for freedom in full sight of its armed guards.

This is one of the faces of extinction. With the strait-jacketing of the Mississippi, with the shaving of its floodplain forests, many bright spirits have fled. Swallow-tailed kites, for example, have been squeezed fourteen hundred miles south in less than a hundred years, all the way from central Minnesota to New Orleans, a very great distance indeed.

What is lost when an organism is extirpated from a range it once inhabited? At a minimum, all the ecological relationships in which it participated and all the functions it provided to the greater community. Over and over, our scientists have documented the consequences of eliminating a predator such as the wolf or the bear from a place, including unintended irruptions of the predator's prey.

When we lost the great bottomland forests of the Mississippi Valley, those millions of acres of self-sustaining, living systems, a suite of other, less visible extinctions and local extirpations, besides the kites, surely occurred as well. There is no way of accounting all those losses.

We know that at least five mass extinctions have occurred in millennia past on our planet, caused by extraordinary catastrophic events such as meteor strikes. To understand how our present situation is uniquely grave, we must pick apart and examine three aspects of extinction: rate, cause, and effect. First, the present rate of extinctions, planetwide, is hundreds or thousands of times higher than in the past, writes Dr. Edward O. Wilson in his book *The Diversity of Life*. Second, today we are experiencing the first mass extinction in the 3.8-billion-year history of life that is caused by a single organism: ourselves, *Homo sapiens*. Finally, the effect of our present exploitation of the earth may be the loss of 15 percent of the world's species within the next ten years! And it is no longer individual species that are currently nudged out of existence but entire ecosystems.

The word *extinction*, the concept of the annihilation of whole life forms, rarely exists in the languages of native peoples, says Chickasaw writer Linda Hogan. "Native people have always had a treaty with the land, that works in both directions; in return for our sustenance, the agreement was that we would never overhunt, overfish, or poison the waters." The settlers of North America, the people who preceded my people, carried no such vow across the Atlantic, introducing instead belief systems and agricultural practices that had subdued the wild things of Europe, including rivers and wolves.

A Great Big Sucking Sound

On Jim Cox's computer screen, the state of Florida was pieced together in patches of fabulous color: khaki and emerald, crimson and lavender, studded and threaded black where lakes and rivers flow. This map—a complex, geographically accurate representation of the state's plant communities, both natural and disturbed—was developed from satellite pictures, a point of view not too different from that of a cruising swallow-tailed kite. The tall stacks of paper on Jim's desk, a nearly dry bathing suit and towel slung over a chair, and his self-effacing manner belied the importance of this conservation biologist's work and his senior authorship of the state wildlife agency's most important work to date, a five-year study entitled Closing the Gaps in Florida's System of Wildlife Conservation Areas.

Using his computer mouse, Jim quickly pointed and clicked on the part of his enormous data set that most interested me, the potential habitat map for kites in Florida. With Ken Meyer's nest locations, Jim had created a relatively detailed picture of where swallow-tailed kites may nest statewide.

Jim homed in on the heart of Florida's kite country, paging through progressively more detailed computer screens. We stared at flat, many-colored versions of the state's mighty rivers and their floodplains, the Apalachicola, the Suwannee, the St. Johns; the vast paper company holdings called Gulf Hammock; and finally, most endangered of all, the sprawling wetlands and prairies of southwest Florida.

"Based on Ken Meyer's estimate of a breeding swallow-tail population in Florida totaling 450–900 pairs, or about 2,000–3,000 individuals, including young of the year and nonbreeding adults," said Jim, "I estimate there are about 1.6 million acres, or 6,400 square kilometers, of potential kite habitat in use by the birds statewide.

"But less than a third of that land—only room enough for about two hundred pairs of kites—is protected on conservation areas of various types, like Big Cypress National Preserve or the Apalachicola National Forest."

That meant there were 4,400 square kilometers, an area the size of Delaware, that the kites could or do use now but that weren't protected. Considering that Florida supported the largest remaining population of swallow-tailed kites in North America, Cox and Meyer knew that the protection of additional habitat was essential if this species was to persist anywhere on the continent.

I wanted to get an idea of what that valuable, vulnerable kite habitat looked like, so I called Kim Dryden, another state wildlife biologist working out of Ft. Myers. Kim was spending her harassed days eking out what protections she could for the wildlife in her region of Florida—the ten southwestern counties, including Collier and Lee, routinely national leaders in population growth. She agreed to give me a quick-and-dirty tour—and her thoughts—on land use changes that may affect swallow-tailed kites in her ten-county territory.

Several weeks later, Kim and I studied an oversized road atlas splayed flat on the hood of her green state pickup at our rendezvous point outside Naples. She suggested a seventy-five-mile driving route that would give me a feel for this landscape and its management issues. Although Kim's manner was entirely professional, I thought there was something wary, something of the wild animals she looks after, in her direct gaze. She was clearly sizing me up. I intuited that in her work she felt cornered, perhaps even battered. I became as interested in this woman as I was in what I hoped she'd teach me.

In Kim's pickup, we hurtled north from Naples on Highway

951, right into the heart of Jim Cox's computer screen, then turned east on State 858, a knife-straight road known locally as Oil Well Grade. The road looked as industrial as its name, all business, although I was pleased to spot a few kestrels, a bluebird or two, occasionally a meadowlark or kingfisher on the telephone wires. Enormous Brazilian pepper bushes barely screened fields and fields of cultivated tomatoes and green peppers from our view.

This southwest slice of the state hosts a peculiar amalgam of land uses: old-style Florida cattle ranching in the interior counties; an enormous vegetable and citrus industry; and galloping urban development along the coast from Sarasota to Marco Island. Land ownership happens on a grand scale in southwest Florida, with a relatively few families or corporations controlling what Kim called "megapieces" of the landscape. In Hendry County, for example, the Alico corporation controls 197 sections of land, more than 125,000 acres. U.S. Sugar owns 46 sections, or 30,000 acres; another 30,000 acres are under the ownership of Hilliard Brothers.

Kim stopped the truck to deliver a minilecture to me. The wind produced by giant produce trucks whizzing by ruffled our hair, and we moved closer to the edge of the road.

"This is Catherine's Island, the documented heart of panther country in Florida," Kim said. It didn't look like it possibly could be.

"Swallow-tailed kites nest here, too. This land still works as decent habitat because remnant bits of pine flatwoods and cypress strands that act as wildlife corridors and refugia remain relatively intact, woven among the farmers' properties."

Kim told me that she was on friendly terms with some of the dozen or more farmers hereabouts. These people know that their business depends on the preservation of the region's water quality, she said, and they have been willing to set aside some of the natural communities that filter and hold the water. Here, farmers are conducting "old-style" vegetable farming, and Kim, speaking for the region's wildlife, could live with it.

She gestured: "Look beyond the squared-off vegetable fields close in. See how those sinuous stands of pine and cypress break the line of the horizon?"

That's where panthers slink and bears roam, she told me. Where kites still nested and successfully foraged, although we hadn't actually seen them so far.

As we continued driving, north of Oil Well Grade, it was a different story. The agricultural development tightened up. Citrus and vegetable fields rolled unbroken over the surface of the land, save for tiny remnant patches of cypress standing tall, out of context, isolated by dikes and ditches choked with exotic vegetation. We passed beehives trucked in to pollinate the citrus bloom. On the left, an army of tomato stakes stood at attention, amid unending acres of propped plants, two feet on center. We passed Bonita Tomato Growers (Farm 5), Serenoa Farm, Harvey Brothers Farm, Silver Strand Farm. Expensive, complex pumps maintain the water table exactly as the growers desire in this geometrically precise agribusiness land.

"Time has been tragic here for 500 years," says the poet Adrienne Rich of our continent. "Before that, the land was not tragic, it was vast, fertile, generous, dangerous, filling the needs of many forms of life. From the first invasion, the first arrogant claiming, it became a tragic land."

I began to want to know how one might affect, even staunch, the crushing forces at work on this landscape, the corporate interests moving over its face as enormous as the summer thunderheads, transforming and dumbing down, reordering the land and the water, demanding. This is the work Kim Dryden does, standing in the face of the great moneyed power every workday. It seemed far beyond my imagined capabilities.

I built on my first question: What is the connection between my own life, its takings and its generosities, and what is happening here?

What is my own culpability in the ransack of this land, I wondered. As a North American, I knew that I was among a privileged 20 percent of the world's people, a sliver of humankind that somehow preempts 67 percent of the planet's resources and generates 75 percent of its pollution and waste. The disappearing of the landscape I visited this day is partially the result of the way people like me live, for example, and what we demand. In this case, fresh orange juice and beefy red tomatoes.

Kim's road tour brought us eventually to a small, sprawling town. Beautiful, brick-edged plantings surrounded a sign that proclaimed "Welcome to Immokalee, My Home." As far as I could tell, this must be where the tomato workers lived, in ghettolike two-story housing surrounded by chain link fence. Their standard of living didn't match the garden club landscaping at the edge of town.

A recent conversation with a Tallahassee acquaintance, Rob Williams, had prepared me for the underbelly of Florida that is Immokalee. Rob said that this was the most "migratory" town in the United States and one of the poorest in all of North America. The attraction for the labor force is the landscape we just drove through: much of the country's winter vegetable crop is grown right here.

"To be a migrant farmworker in Immokalee (and there are many thousands of them)," Rob told me, "you are by definition poor, oppressed, desperate, or all three." Rob Williams knows his subject well. He is a lawyer for Florida Rural Legal Services who worked on behalf of immigrant farmworkers in Immokalee for sixteen years. He chose to live here partly for proximity to Corkscrew Swamp, a nationally known Audubon sanctuary, because Rob is nearly as passionate about birds as he is about his clients.

Rob saw the racial composition of the farmworkers shift continuously during his tenure in Immokalee, from Mexican and African Americans and poor whites from all over the rural south to Haitians, Guatemalans, and, most recently, Maya and other indigenous peoples from central Mexico.

"Those who immigrate here from traditional societies, such as the Chiapas Indians, lose a lot, even if they find some small material gain. Many die or get killed, or leave their families, or simply never go home. In their home villages, impoverished as they were, they were somebody. Here, they are just fruit pickers, just dirt, basically, in the eyes of the ruthless corporations they work for."

As a legal advocate and as a birdwatcher, Rob witnessed the parallel effects of agribusiness on farmworkers and wildlife alike in southwest Florida. His litany of places broken and lost in the name of profit is an old, heartbreaking story.

It suddenly felt essential to try to locate myself in the stream of people moving to this continent—and to discover how our comfortable lives transmogrify into the abuses before me. I had given little thought to where I had really come from, beyond my nuclear family, and suddenly felt, as the poet Adrienne Rich observes, as if we had "emerged from nowhere . . . as if each of us has lived, thought and worked without any historical past or contextual present."

When I asked, my father sent me an enormous copy of our family tree, and through his careful research and engineer's script, I began to trace the tracks of who I am, at least on the paternal side. His parents, my Grandma and Grandpa, Charles and Alice Hunziker Isleib, were both born in Paterson, New Jersey, just before the turn of the twentieth century. They were nowhere near when the great virgin woodlands of the South and the whole of the Mississippi Valley were felled of their

ancient timber and the swallow-tailed kites lost to that part of
their range and ivory-billed woodpeckers forced into extinction.
They had not yet moved twenty miles from Ellis Island, where
their own parents, in a hopelessly braided torrent of immigrant
longing, had streamed into New York City from Germany and
Switzerland, from England and Northern Ireland (and of those
lives we know almost nothing.) We were not yet here when the
first trees fell. Still, in the present, surely we must bear some
responsibility for those losses set into motion before our births.

For my benefit, in the course of our conversation, Rob
Williams had ticked off, precisely, his most dramatic swallow-
tailed kite encounters, in Tikal, Guatemala; Costa Rica; Mexico;
Corkscrew. "And I saw swallow-tailed kites every day in
Immokalee, for years," Rob told me. "Just like you'd see Mississippi kites in Tallahassee—in twos or threes, flying high overhead."

But Rob never forgot the presence of kites at the funeral of
Father Richard Sanders at Our Lady of Guadalupe Catholic
Church in Immokalee in the mid-1980s.

"Father Sanders championed the immigrant community. He
was a guy with tremendous burdens and responsibilities, tending to a huge parish of tremendously poor people. Other priests
had come and gone under such stressful demands, but Father
Sanders stayed, serving his community, and he was deeply beloved by the parishioners.

"It was very unexpected, and an enormous loss to the community, when he died of a heart attack at only age forty-seven.
At the funeral mass for Father Sanders, the crowds were so big
they overflowed out of the tiny church into the churchyard and
the street. They had to bring in microphones and loudspeakers
so that everyone could hear. The mass was conducted in three
languages: Creole, Spanish, and English.

"We were outdoors, under the pines around the church, when suddenly, as if in tribute, a pair of swallow-tailed kites flew very low over the crowds. I'll never forget that moment."

The dreams that shaped my own people and their fellow immigrants to North America, limited as they were by their hard lives, did not allow these new residents to let the landscape and inhabitants of this continent speak to them. They were living out the perception of a great exodus from Europe, looking for the promised land, as Sister Miriam MacGillis says, with tragic cost to the continent.

My father has gathered together priceless black-and-white images of our immigrant forebears: Julius Caesar Hunziker and his wife, Elizabeth Hunziker; Charles Frederick Isleib and his wife, Mary Miller, and Jacob Isleib, father of Charles. The reproductions are exquisite in detail, the faces inscrutable. All the men are thin and dark and bearded. The women, stern and heavy and soft bodied. There is no softness in their return gaze. I do not see their faces for this first time ever and feel a rush of ancestry fill up my empty places. I do not know them.

"I am so glad for the pictures, Dad," I said into the phone, happy with these riches, the names and images of the people who directly preceded me, newly born into my hands nearly a century after their deaths, when I was just short of fifty years old myself.

"But don't you just wish you knew their life stories?" I asked him. He did and agreed that these bare names and dates seemed a tease. We were impatient with so little—just names and lines on a genealogy chart. I wanted to know: What did they fiercely dream? How did they define themselves, and what were their most private imaginings for themselves? How had softness come to be traded for survival? Art and expression for order? Living landscapes for unthinkable excess?

I do know one thing: how close in cellular memory my people were at one time to bare survival—because I had stood at the stove myself as a child and watched the hungry satisfaction with which Nana steamed fat white dumplings and beef stew in the heavy gray pressure cooker and how my grandmother Alice would cluck her tongue in uncommon anticipation as she cooked corned beef and carrots, pink meat that fell away in strings from itself, and sauerbraten and even the organ meats, the kidneys and tongue and liver of cows.

"I ached for the ignorance of my kind," writes Barbara Kingsolver, "who always seemed to arrive in paradise thinking only of our next meal."

Once landed in North America, my people began to scrabble for purchase on the middle class. By the time I was born, the bread we ate was sturdy and substantial; it was rye or pumpernickel or whole wheat, never the white Wonder Bread some of my classmates carried in their school lunches, smeared with mustard and small shelves of bologna. I knew that you could compress a slice of that Wonder bread into a single thumb-sized dough ball and eat it in one bite—it had that little substance—because I had done so with a whole loaf of that bread, one slice after another, a souvenir from a fifth-grade field trip to the Sunbeam factory in Newark. There wouldn't have been another way to know. And every day of my child-life, we would wake to five tiny glasses of orange juice lined up for us on the kitchen counter, my father's gift, what he mixed and poured for us before he boarded the 7 a.m. train to New York City.

It comes to this: even if no stories remain at all, if all I ever hold is this clutch of ancient photographs (which seems likely), still I must be the living nerve ending of all their living.

As we headed west out of town on Highway 846, Kim informed me that we were approaching the Immokalee Rise, one of five major physiographic regions in southwest Florida.

We joked about the thin air as we moved several feet higher above sea level, although there was no perceptible change in elevation at all.

Besides supporting a profitable cattle industry, the interior ranchlands of the Immokalee Rise were historically an immense, little-known country, composed of unfenced, open range up until the 1940s. This vast mosaic of stark and beautiful prairies interspersed with pinewoods and cypress swamps has bred a veritable bestiary of rarities. Jim Cox had told me that, in terms of maintaining several wide-ranging species that constitute an important part of wildlife diversity in Florida, this region, the southwest, may be the most important in the state. It harbors the only stable population of panther found east of the Mississippi; the only stable population of black bear south of Lakeland; the greatest concentration of Audubon's crested caracaras in all of the United States; core populations of sandhill cranes, swallow-tailed kites, and burrowing owls; and important foraging and nesting habitat for large, diverse colonies of Florida's specialty—wading birds.

Although many Florida biologists speak with a sort of reverence about southwest Florida, confirming its rich biodiversity, their words are often overlaid with quiet desperation: they know much of it is about to go under the bulldozer's blade. Despite its outstanding biological richness, the region falls just below the statewide average in percentage of lands under conservation ownership. And Hendry and Glades fall well below the statewide average for individual counties.

Kim put it bluntly: "There's a great big sucking sound coming from southwest Florida. All the listed species are going down the drain."

The primary culprit is citrus. Since its introduction to the St. Augustine region of north Florida in the sixteenth century, that industry has been moving south, seeking permanent refuge from winter frosts.

"It wouldn't be so bad if the groves were interspersed with

less intensive land uses," said Kim. "We know that some animals, like deer and panther, can coexist under those circumstances. It's when you have an unbroken twelve square miles of citrus production, and it doesn't vary over a twenty-year period, that it is virtually sterile for wildlife."

During the 1980s and '90s, landowners of a stunning eighty thousand hectares of the Immokalee Rise had received the required permits to convert their land to groves by the year 2000, with a projected production value of $380 million.

With this kind of money at stake, I wasn't completely surprised when Kim said she was regularly threatened, bullied, or cursed by the developers for whose plans she must address potential effects on wildlife.

"There's just no polite way to comment on these types of impacts," she concluded with the humorless laugh that punctuated much of her conversation. "In many cases, citrus groves require a basic 'nuking' of the landscape.

"And you know, developers say to me, you're going to force me to have to eliminate things. I say, look, you can kill it now, shoot it in the head; or kill it slowly, destroy its habitat with your project. Either way it will be just as dead in five years."

Despite Kim's professional appearance—regulation sage green trousers, tan polyester-blend uniform shirt, and sturdy work boots—a barely suppressed rage sneaked through her careful words. That, and her blunt honesty, probably didn't always work to her advantage in her dealings with the "regulated" public.

We talked about the incredible turnover of employees in jobs comparable to Kim's in the sister resource agencies. Kim maintained that it is the scale of land conversion that causes conservationists to burn out quickly in southwest Florida. People just can't take the pressure and the loss. And so there's little commitment to the region and virtually no collective memory of the original landscape.

We kept driving, through miles of pastureland, dotted with cabbage palm and forested sloughs.

We learned that it was my grandfather, Charles Isleib, who led our family's struggle out of the working class to the middle class and my own father and uncle who finished that for us: so that now we manage and supervise, teach and write, instead of making things with our hands. I noticed that only the men's vocations form the strong outlines of the family story.

I thought of what I had experienced of my own father's work. What if I were not here in southwest Florida, staggered by the impacts of industrial agriculture and urbanization on kite habitat, but rather in Sudbury, Ontario, forty years back, where my father's lifelong employer was ravaging with its mining practices that part of the continent? Wouldn't I have a better picture of how the underpinnings of my life have participated in the annihilation of the landscape's natural cover?

"I loved working with hot metal," my father told me recently when I asked about his first job out of college. "And my company needed men who understood iron work. It was a really exciting time for me." This, my dad's first job, involved tracking the progress of furnaces full of steel in the melting shops—the smelters—of the International Nickel Company in Ashland County, Kentucky. Better known as Inco, this company takes more than forty times the weight of the Eiffel Tower each year from the living ground, even today.

His supervisors must have seen how this young man's enthusiasm would serve them in marketing the ores they were digging—and still excavate and process—from Ontario's Sudbury basin and now all over the world, for they quickly moved him up into white-collar work.

As a young child, my primary experience of what my father did for a living revolved around whether he was home or

out of town. So often, his work for money required travel. The
nickel ore was mined in Canada. The markets he was charged to
develop were all over the United States.

Our family lost emotional ground when he was gone, even as
our material lifestyle gradually improved.

He saw how we hovered over his suitcase—both the packing
of it and the unpacking. As he polished his shoes or brushed the
lint off his good dark suit, we'd count out three, four, or five
white shirts, lightly starched, with the dry cleaner's cardboard
ring holding his collars straight and stiff; an equal number of
black socks, rolled; and a couple of conservative ties. One or
another of us four children might miss the ritual of his packing,
but we all gathered round on the white chenille bedspread to
check for little gifts he'd bring us back from Chicago, Kansas
City, or Detroit. He'd try to compensate for his time away by
taking us one at a time on business trips or into New York City
to visit his workplace.

In my father's high-perched Wall Street office, there
was only one tangible sign of the nature of his work. Every
visit, while he talked on the phone or to his secretary, I would
turn it in my hands trying to read its meaning: a thick triangular
Plexiglass paperweight, which displayed at its core a small
chunk of nickel ore. Distributed around it, like bits of sun ray,
were the ore's constituent parts, labeled: copper, cobalt, gold,
nickel, selenium, and other primary metals.

"Every day, without being aware of it, you are touched by
products made from Inco metals," reads the company's literature, even today. "Inco metals live behind the scenes, used
mostly as constituents of other products: coins, stainless steel
kitchen sinks, aircraft parts, batteries and endless more. Modern
industrial society could not exist without them."

We were not oppressed or physically worn like the miners or
the foundry workers. We were not poor: my father earned a
solid middle-class wage. We were not damaged like the de-

stroyed mountains that were mined nor choked like the people of Sudbury who breathed the massive metal smelter's air.

The price we paid was that we could not know the whole story of what supported us. The cost to us was separation, in all its varieties. Our most personal price as a family was our agreement to uproot and resettle at the company's behest, to tolerate the absences of our father.

I am in ninth grade, about to begin high school in Birmingham, Michigan, where we have lived for the past three years. I have friends I love, I've adapted to the Midwest, finally, after our last Inco-induced transplant from New Jersey and have survived the worst of adolescence—figuring out how to fit in.

My parents call me into the living room. I stand next to a wine-colored wingback chair, keeping its back between my body and theirs, sensing bad news.

"We're being transferred," my mother said. "We're going back home!"

A body blow. "No!" I screamed. "You can't make me. Every person I care about in the world is here, now. There's nothing for me in New Jersey, absolutely nothing at all."

I pleaded. They reasoned. I lashed out in anguish and fury. I imagine now that their hearts broke for me.

But I was only fourteen; I had no real power at all. Everyone said it wasn't the end of the world.

Transferring, transplanting, was the price we all had to pay, just like enlisted men, if we (my father) were to advance, stay with the company, stay in favor. Each time, the carrots were better schools; a bigger, brand-new house; enough bedrooms for each of us to have our own. But in the end, after a lifetime of cheerful obedience and loyalty, the company "downsized" my father, some years before he was actually set to retire.

❧

My father's work simply reflected the extreme invest-
ment in mining the planet, and he himself, a very disposable
part of our country's economy, an economy that cannot last
because it is predicated on the removal of nonrenewable resources from the land and water, in all their forms.

My father always tried to do good within the sphere of
influence the company allowed him. His enthusiasm, his inven-
tive bent, his love of teamwork were appreciated among his
peers. He did his dead-level best to do the job laid out for
him—find new ways to use nickel and convince other manufac-
turers to buy it in ever increasing quantities. His opinion about
whether all the requisite mining was a good idea—made sense
for the highest good—was never solicited.

Among my father's legacies from his decades with the International Nickel Company are a comfortable retirement, several
children launched even higher into the middle class than he was
able to manage for himself, and frequent nightmares.

Time and again, in the dark hours of sleep, he is fired from
his job. Over and over, he wakes my stepmother, legs thrashing,
shouting, in a sweat—he relives the fear that kept him moving,
of failing the family he loved and himself.

"Now there is some native range—flatwoods prairie,"
said Kim, pointing out the window to a vista of widely spaced
pine with palmetto in the understory. Cattle moved about, grazing on tall grasses. Some stood belly deep in small oval wetlands
under the hot sun.

The more common scenario for cattle grazing is the same
scene minus the pines (trucked away to lumber mills), with just
a few scattered palms and oaks ("And it's still better habitat than
sugarcane and citrus," said Kim). The next, more intensive
operations, with increased cattle production and profitability,
again involve the same landscape, but with palmetto and other
woody vegetation leveled and disked and native herbaceous
cover replaced with planted range grass.

"This is one group of landowners with a piece of that collective memory of the land we were talking about," Kim mused. "The cattlemen. There are families who have lived and worked this land for many, many years. Keeping their ranches somewhat intact would provide a lot of security to the region's wildlife. Rangeland is one of those categories where people can make a living and maintain a certain contingent of the original wildlife as well."

But burdensome inheritance taxes and rising land values are pressing the landowners to go for the maximum developable acreage. Intensive, wildlife-sterile citrus conversion looks more and more attractive. The state clearly can't buy it all. It seems, then, that the future of swallow-tailed kites and all kinds of other wildlife may lie in working out agreements and easements with these large landowners, figuring out how to make it worth their while to keep their land semiwild.

At day's end, we still hadn't seen any kites, though they were known to nest there. I found myself unexpectedly drawn to this mosaic of rangeland and native biota. Back at my car, we said our goodbyes. Kim's gaze was as intense as a searchlight, and in her parting words I read the subtext of her sorrow and her rage and her impotence at all the losses of wildlands and wild creatures.

"You guys up in Tallahassee look at south Florida and say it's all gone. It's not. I didn't mean to get so attached to this place, but I'm not giving up."

We shook hands, and she was gone, flying up the road in her green pickup to handle "an eagle problem" in Punta Gorda.

As I began my own long drive north, toward home, I thought: my journeys after kites make no sense if I cannot draw my own life along into coherent relationship with what I see happening here in Florida, my chosen home. Yet I am confronting landscape-level transformations buttressed with fortunes and anticipations at a scale beyond my normal frame of reference. My people have never owned large landscapes like the

ones I have seen in southwest Florida. We are the middle
people; we are suspended between the immigrants of Immokalee, Florida, and Paterson, New Jersey, and the cloistered
Collier land barons who bend this place to their bidding. Still,
our bodies and our agreements to do the midlevel work must
somehow hold this whole structure in place. There are only a
handful, maybe several dozen, Kim Dryden types willing and
able to play David to the Goliath corporations sculpting—even
"terraforming"—our world. What is my part to do? What is
ours? What is possible?

The Way We Love a Journey

No time to travel to Ken's south Florida field sites this season. He hasn't got room for observers anyway: his crew has grown large along with the complexity of his research. But on the basis of friendship and a long, shared fascination with kites, Ken and I met for lunch in Lake City, fifty miles north of his home, ninety miles east of mine.

I didn't mind the drive, a knife-straight shot east on Interstate-10. All I had to do was keep the car headed east, with an eye open for speeding semitrucks. My body knew the drill. Sit still and press the gas pedal.

Big green signs marked my progress across the panhandle of Florida. Monticello, Madison, Perry. The Tallahassee public radio station gave way to crackle and static around Greenville. I wouldn't catch anything like it unless I were to head all the way to Jacksonville or south to Gainesville. So I dropped back into my thoughts. Like my father, like my mother, I am plenty familiar with that peculiarly American pastime of hurtling through space while remaining perfectly inert in the body; this is what we do in our cars, on our sofas, in front of our television, with our computers. We are a restless people; we do not clump together for long in any one place.

Aside from coping with periodic relocations by my father's company, my family traveled widely and by choice on almost every summer and school vacation. We'd prepare for days; my father designed ambitious itineraries and boxy rooftop bins to stretch the packing space for six people and a German shepherd dog. My job was to assemble and refresh the contents of a first aid kit in a heavy metal ammunition box my father had stashed in the attic. Mom was always in charge of the food. The first night on the road, nearly any trip, we'd load paper plates to sagging with her oven-baked chicken, homemade potato salad, and crusty hard rolls. Licking the buttery bread crumbs from my fingers in the Chevrolet's middle seat, a stack of library books at my feet and weeks on the road ahead of us, I felt myself enmeshed in all I knew of comfort in the world.

"Surely as any river, we exist in movement," said the writer William Kittredge. It's true: there is little that many of us North Americans love more than travel and the planning of travel. In that place between places, we can hang in a sort of contentment, the best it seems we can fashion. Sitting alone or side by side, facing forward, moving forward, we are comfortable in the motion more than in the moment, clear of the haunt of the past place, hopeful that the new will be all we desire. Driving, we work at the rent fabric of our lives and the lives of those we love, mulling, worrying. Projecting outward what we might attend to in ourselves.

Driving in cars, flying in airplanes, watching screens are not in any way programmed into our human animal bodies, I think to myself, squirming in the car seat, fiddling with the cruise control. What is built in is the heavy weight of a child on our laps or our backs, the grip of a hoe or a shovel, the feel of a long day's striding in our thighs, the sound of the wind, the rain, the bird and the frog, the stir of the fire.

Finally, a sign informed me I was just two miles from the southbound exit to Lake City. I steered gratefully into a Wendy's hamburger joint where we'd agreed to meet, the least offensive of the interstate exit offerings.

Ken beat me—I pulled into an empty slot next to his forest green pickup truck.

Shouldering through the fingerprint-smudged glass door, I picked out Ken and his five-year-old son, Cameron, at a corner table, heads bent close over a toy.

"It was naptime at our house, and Cameron's too big for that now," Ken explained, as I settled myself at their table. The boy watched me with the round blue eyes of his father and a shy sweet manner, then emptied out a sack of crayons and colored pencils on the small square table as his father began to talk.

"It's such a switch this year, you wouldn't believe it," said Ken, unfolding a map of the continents of North and South America. He handed Cameron an identical copy to color, and the boy pushed aside his French fries, beginning with Belize and a burnt umber crayon.

"I just turn on the computer and the satellite tells me where my birds are, every eight hours. I don't even have to lace a boot, or break a sweat." He grinned.

Turns out the first thing the birds do postbreeding, Ken said, is "rocket" around the southeastern United States.

"What I see now is that the young of the year and adults whose nesting attempts fail spend the second half of the summer basically wandering. They cover very large distances in very short times in unpredictable directions for unpredictable lengths of time," he summarized, grimacing at the bitter dregs of coffee in his paper cup.

"Through the satellite data, I'm watching how individual kites jump around the big river systems of the Southeast, even in the course of a single day. They'll travel between Lake Okeechobee and Everglades National Park on one day and return the next."

As Ken interprets his data, not only are these kites checking out good foraging habitat, but they are also mapping. Mapping their natal territory, the place where they were born. Where they will return to raise their own chicks in a season or two. Unlike less mobile species, kites learn early to move around an enormous ecological neighborhood or territory and don't imprint on a single home site. Home is an enormous tract of landscape they come to know as you and I might know the floor plans of our own houses.

"I have no idea exactly how they're doing it," said Ken. "Maybe using visual cues or working with magnetic fields. But I can tell you they are extraordinarily wide ranging; their flight movements are unbelievably quick and efficient."

Ken Meyer and other conservation biologists who study migratory species have urgent reasons to study migration—they want to assess, especially, what the conditions are like where "our" birds overwinter. When Ken began his kite work in 1988, almost nothing was known about the distribution and status of the bird in South America. The route they took south was entirely unknown. They were never observed on migration counts. The only previous clue to the swallow-tail's international migration came thirty years ago when a metal leg band placed on a young kite in south Florida was sent back to the United States from southeastern Brazil, where the bird had been shot and killed. That bird's carcass was found near the area where Meyer's team tracked the southernmost extent of the migration last year. And it turns out the kites were almost never seen along their migration route because—as Meyer learned in 1996—the birds migrate early, beginning in July, and they don't travel in large, noticeable groups.

I parted company with the Meyer men, regretfully. My head was full of facts, trying to piece together the kites' journeys with mine. How does their travel differ from ours, from mine, I began to wonder. Are we the same, then, two species simply, inexorably pulled by new vistas and broad distances? Perhaps my urge to wander, my inability to just stay home, arises from the braiding together of a hodgepodge of mobile bloodlines, even though surely at one time, before scarcity, each had an affinity to an ancestral landscape.

I know that I am descended from travelers, uprooted so many times that we no longer recognize or reroot in a permanent single home. We are people who long for the next trip, the next diversion in the weather, the landscape, the possibility of things. "I can't wait for . . . !" Or "If only we could . . . !" It's not just my desire, either; it's the great American ache. This migratory urge has little to do with follow-through or time in the trenches. A fear of being bored feeds it, and a desire for instant gratification. A desire to consummate with something other than what is. It doesn't help you learn new languages or stay married or knit a sweater.

The trouble is that all over this overpopulated planet, diasporas of desperate proportions are happening, from Mongolia to Central America, people moving to the city or to the country, dodging war and famine; you can almost feel the planet wobble with displacements. But for our part, we in well-off North America can't say we are looking for clean water, food, or even safety, generally. We drive, we fly, we consume as much as we do because we are driven by needs we can't name, hungers that collectively have a monstrous effect on our earth. For us—the planet's well-to-do—the whole earth has become our range. The costs of our wandering and our consumption are so high. And there seem to be no visible mechanisms built into our biologies to stop us, no intrinsic self-limiting. In the middle and upper classes, many of us have two or three homes; each family certainly has one car per driver; and the excesses of our lifestyles are broadcast by television to every country on earth.

Less than three months after its birth, a young swallow-tail migrates far to the south. The young birds leave Florida three or four weeks after their parents, but they travel twice as fast. They move about ninety miles a day, compared with about fifty a day for adults.

"I have no idea how they do it," Ken says.

On Ken's map of the Americas, North and South, he showed me what the satellites (sailing five hundred miles above the planet) were reporting about our swallow-tails. It was a far cry from the old days. In 1996, Ken's research ratcheted up many notches with the advent of satellite transmitter technology.

The satellite data show that the kites, traveling in small groups, hop from south Florida to Cuba and then to the Yucatán Peninsula. They cruise the coastal lowland forests of eastern Central America, switch to the Pacific coast in Colombia, and dive through a pass in the Andes where the mountains narrow at the town of Pasto. By late fall, the birds settle into large communal roosts in forested edges of the Pantanal, a massive wetland comparable to the Everglades, at the Bolivian border in southern Brazil.

"The kites take their time getting down there," Ken said. "I suspect most of their wintering behavior is essentially moving about, possibly following emerging swarms of insects, much as we see them do here in late summer.

"The motto of the kite might be this: keep a close eye on your 'conspecifics' because they might be feeding on something good!"

If you are getting all your needs met in one place, you have no reason to move. Migration is a perilous pastime: it's got to be worth it, or you wouldn't even try. Still, it's not uncommon for animals to migrate, to wander nomadically. Birds aren't the only animals that do it. Caribou, trout, land crabs, salamanders, whales, and sea lions also migrate, tracking predictable, valuable resources, particularly food and water.

The phenomenon of bird migration probably has its roots in irregular wanderings. Large, extremely mobile birds, like hawks, vultures, and kites, are well equipped to move about in response to local food conditions. Scientists believe that the tendency to migrate becomes genetically incorporated and that as a species or population continues this behavior, it begins to hone more of the attributes it needs to succeed as a migrant. Many of the birds that migrate—thrushes, warblers, vireos, and many others—originated in the tropics. Migration to a summer range in the Northern Hemisphere helps them avoid competing with year-round residents for nesting space, food, and water.

Most of Florida's present avifauna was established by the invasion of modern bird species that had evolved elsewhere. When kites and other birds of prey were evolving, in the Pleistocene (15,000 to 1 million years ago), much of Florida, the Bahamas, and the coastal plain of the southeastern United States was submerged. The speciation of swallow-tailed kites on the planet predated the emergence of this Florida landscape from the sea. Like most of the state's 165 native breeding birds, they have arrived from elsewhere. Their godly attributes and effortless flight were not specifically shaped over the long reach of our tropical peninsula. But when, exactly, this species became established on the North American continent is not known. The birds' air-filled bones have left no fossil record. Ken, my conservative scientist, will say only that it is likely kites have been congregating at the Okeechobee roost for twenty years. So we can't know when the lives of humans and swallow-tailed kites first intersected in the southeastern United States. Perhaps the first human eyes that followed the flight of swallow-tails were Paleoindians, the first people to live in Florida, a good twelve thousand years ago.

Fisheating Creek

One sticky August sunrise, a woman named Susan Ettchey helped me shove a battered aluminum canoe into Fisheating Creek just where it intersects State Road 78 on Lake Okeechobee's west flank. As we ducked under the highway bridge and paddled west, the creek stretched wide, buffered from the pasturelands on either bank by broad rafts of white water lily and pink-flowering smartweed. A purple gallinule and her long-legged chick clung to pairs of tall flower stalks of duck potato. I could see the chick struggle with the linked problems of maintaining balance and evaluating the extent of threat we posed. All around us, the landscape stretched flat and hot as a skillet.

I had come to try to find Fort Center, a remote archaeological site, which had intrigued me with its mystery and inaccessibility for the past several years. It was difficult to reach at that time because it sat on land held privately by the Lykes family, an empire of cattle-ranching, food-processing, citrus, land, and natural gas interests; the family brooked no trespassers on any of the 227,000 acres of Glades County property it owned. Susan promised to bring me at least within sight of the ancient mounds of Fort Center, although it was illegal to disembark and walk on the area.

"The Lykes keep a real tight grip on this part of Florida," Susan told me. "I know several folks who have tried to picnic or explore near Fort Center, as we all once did, freely. They ended up arrested by Lykes security people and never saw their canoe again."

What I knew about Fort Center I'd learned from archaeology texts. More than two thousand years of human occupation have been documented in this low-lying country of savannah and saw grass marsh in the Lake Okeechobee floodplain, on the banks of this very creek. Ancient cultures constructed gigantic earthen circles, mounds, and an elaborate mortuary platform over a shallow pond for the purposes of complex ritual. The ceremonial platform especially intrigued me because, according to William Sears, the archaeologist who originally excavated the Fort Center site, 150 vertical pine posts beautifully carved in the likenesses of eagles, hawks, wading birds, bears, and other wild animals stood vigil over the community dead. Moreover, middens on this site contained very little bird bone, indicating that birds were not eaten, Sears suggested, because they were probably considered sacred. I'd been wondering if any of those carved birds were swallow-tailed kites and, if so, what they may have signified to those long-ago peoples.

What I wanted to know was if there were any relationship, no matter how far-fetched, between this ancient ceremonial site and the enormous premigratory roost of swallow-tailed kites gathering up only a mile or two south of where we paddled. It was an old question: asking ruins to speak.

Susan and I worked our way upriver to the west a couple of miles. Gradually, the channel constricted, the marshes evaporated, and only an occasional leafy slough snaked into the land, now on the right, now the left. I felt there was something unnatural about this stretch of the creek, how abruptly the land transitioned to water, how only planted pasture grass spilled into the water here and there. None of the softening diversity of native flora that we had seen closer to the lake. Still, we passed lots of alligators, all sizes. The paddling offered an unre-markable, steady accompaniment to our easy conversation in the canoe. Susan was working on a screenplay about the Second Seminole War, and she recounted her story in enough interest-ing detail to pass the time between Mileposts 2 and 4. I pointed out the birds we passed: two spotted sandpipers bobbing their way along a sandy bank, a single little blue heron, a smattering of white and glossy ibis. Her distance vision was bad, Susan said, so she had trouble picking out the swallow-tailed kites rising in slow boils off the hot upland pastures, mixed sometimes with vultures and a hawk or two. I felt sorry for her, having to miss them. From the back of the canoe, I watched the brown skin of her back begin to shine as the hours passed and the temperature rose.

Certain characteristics of birds have always impressed humans: their swift motion, sudden apparition and disappearance, and the suggestion of communion with higher powers implicit in their powers of flight. In many cultures, eagles, hawks, and kites are widely associated with sky gods. One of the most persistent motifs regarding birds in nearly all mythologies and folklore is their ability to speak and be understood by humans. To be able to understand the language of birds was viewed as equivalent to being able to converse with the gods, and augury, one branch of this communication, has been developed and employed on a daily basis among indigenous peoples all over the globe. This art of observing and interpreting signs of approval or disapproval sent by the gods regarding human undertakings has been described by an Iban tribesman from Borneo: "These birds of augury, they indicate to us things that are hurtful and things that are not; but if we do not understand their language, if we do not heed them, then we suffer."

For the Iban people, the messages are brought from the gods by only a select few "sacred" species. The Iban believe that it is important to understand that it is not the augur birds or their messages that produce results, either good or bad, but rather how humans respond to the communication. One thing I feel quite sure of: if there were only seven sacred birds among the hundreds that spend parts of their lives in Florida, the swallow-tailed kite would surely rank at the top of the list.

What is it, I wonder, that our own birds would tell us, perhaps are telling us, if only we could understand? To my disappointment, a swallow-tailed kite has never spoken to me. Or rather, I have never understood myself to be spoken to by such a bird. The way I have understood kites is through their unexpected and propitious appearances, surging over and past me at a time when I was rolling a question around in my head. At those moments, I impart great significance to the thing I am doing or pondering at the moment of the "visitation." I believe these simple, crude noticings on my part must parallel the beginnings of systems of augury. Others have told me of similar experiences. A friend, lying in her bed near an uncurtained window, debating about a problematic marriage, was deeply surprised by the fleet shadow and then the unmistakable body of a kite passing through her process like an airborne wraith-messenger. In some way, the happenstance appearance of such a remarkable bird informed her decision, a prophecy.

But we are not taught to give weight to these things in our culture. Most of us do not believe in animal omens; nor is the power of the natural world woven very tightly into whatever religious frameworks we are raised in here in North America. We see ourselves apart from, so independent of the living planet we inhabit. Such separation robs us of the rich contributions the rest of the living entities might offer our often troubled selves.

Fairies were the only winged creatures to whom I directed my childhood prayers. Sarah, my best friend in kindergarten, assured me that, under the right circumstances, it was possible to hatch brilliantly hued fairies from pinecones, and I wanted that more than I could speak. Sarah was sandy haired and as rumpled as a golden puppy, her serious face mapped with freckles, a reliable source, I felt sure. It was her certainty regarding spirit that drew me to her house after school as much as the fairies she promised.

We sat together on her wooden porch, our heads bent over a

plastic-lidded palette of watercolor paints and a basket of tightly closed cones we had just collected from her grassy back-yard.

"All you have to do is pick the color you want your fairy's wings to be," she explained, pressing her wet brush against the bright yellow paint. I chose purple for my first cone, coating and recoating each brown scale with my thick-handled brush.

"How do you *know* we'll get fairies?" I asked.

"My sister saw them herself and told me exactly what to do," she said firmly, demonstrating how to hold the cone by its woody stem so I wouldn't smear the paint. "You just have to pray."

We lined up the wet cones (like a set of crude Easter eggs) on sheets of newspaper to dry while we outfitted two makeshift nests, cardboard shoe boxes lined with thick cotton from her family's upstairs medicine cabinet. "To incubate," she said. "You know, like birds."

I believed in the possibilities of Sarah's fairies as long as I could, but at home, away from her faith, the magic box hidden under my bed seemed only a messy container of paint-splotched cotton and ordinary pinecones.

As a child, I spent part of every summer vacation with my family at the New Jersey shore and the Outer Banks of North Carolina. Using *Peterson's Field Guide to the Birds of Eastern North America* and my father's binoculars, we identified the simpler species (willet and sanderling) and learned how to tell a gull from a tern. We were always happy by the sea. But for the most part, both the ocean and the forested mountain where we lived were simply the backdrop against which we played out our preoccupied personal concerns. Myth, omen, spiritual connection with nature never entered our conscious minds. I think you must be steeped in the intimate knowledge of your landscape for augury to be even possible. If you have not learned when an animal might be present or absent, nor its name, nor any of its habits, then you can hardly expect to base decisions on its appearance or activities when you do happen to see it.

As a teen, I often walked among the trees on the wooded mountain behind our house, winter, fall, spring, trying to sort out my complicated adolescent emotions. I'd let myself out the back door after school, longing a magnetized compass point and me the metal, pulled toward longing, calling it by the names of my father's God. I did not hear a reply. I was hoping for intervention, for revelation, for guidance, maybe most of all for peace. The woods were quiet. Nothing spoke back. I touched the trees, but I did not know how to communicate with the sacred; I knew only my lack, my desire, my undressed want. I would sing hymns, the only sacred music I knew. I wished for fairies, for tree spirits, but without much hope. I was calling on the sacred and could not see that it stood before my very eyes. I could not hear anyone answer; if they did, it was in too faint a whisper. But perhaps it was enough: I always since have wanted to be among trees. Perhaps I caught the barest whiff of what must have been ours, a connection to nature muffled and devalued over the centuries.

Most of us today know so little of the natural world, our home; only the fewest names, and so little of the miraculous work of their community. Tree. Bird. Grass. Lake. River. Cloud. We are reduced to the language of babies, primitive, basic, and we are not taught by our inherited religions that these things are primary, sacred, of the Spirit. We are unlike native peoples, for example, the Koyukon of the Pacific Northwest, who have two hundred words for snow, each expressive of a meaningful variation. Our modern intimacy is with our human culture and its virtual realities, not the living planet of which we are simply a part.

While our minds drifted in private thoughts, Susan and I paddled steadily upstream through the wide-open landscape. Spreading live oak trees and scrubby wax myrtles punctuated the fields. The sun pummeled our heads, and my shoulders ached with an unaccustomed pull from wielding a borrowed, too-short paddle. A green blur on the south bank of the creek finally materialized into thick hammock—oaks, tall cabbage palm, and wild citrus filling up the understory with limey, dark green fragrance.

This is it, Susan told me.

I drew the canoe closer to the shady bank and peered into the little forest's dark interior. Very mysterious, and very off limits. We tied our canoe to a rough branch that stretched over the current, and we peeled oranges into the bottom of the boat. I wiggled the plastic wrapper off a stick of mozzarella cheese, and Susan spooned out leftovers from a small Tupperware container. We were glad for the cold water in our small red cooler and for Gatorade, as well. The entire time we ate, a crow called from a high tree on the opposite bank, like a sentinel, I thought. If I were Lykes security, that's exactly where I'd post a guard myself. Nevertheless, as we unloosed the bowline and began the drift back toward Lake Okeechobee, I made Susan stop when I spotted a soft, high green mound several hundred yards from shore on the oak-studded bank. It was clearly an intentional mound; it projected a sense of "old" to me in some way I wanted to believe. It couldn't be a levee or waste soil. Braving the invisible forces of Lykes, I raced to the emerald summit of the hillock, paused ever so briefly, longing to stay and absorb whatever I could soak in through my body of this place.

Susan gestured nervously from the bank of the creek, and I lost my nerve, sprinting to the safety of the canoe. No answers for me there that day.

One Sunday morning, as my seven-year-old David and I swept the beautiful handmade brick walk leading to our front steps, he stopped short and said: "Mom, when I've got one cousin who believes in aliens, and one who is a Christian and believes in Jesus, what am I supposed to think?"

It broke my heart to think I had given him so little spiritual framework. It had felt right to have him baptized in a Protestant church at age two, and his father didn't object, even though his favorite reading material on spiritual matters was a periodic magazine called the *Skeptical Inquirer*. It had been my pregnancy with David that drew me back to the church of my childhood, but even with its loving community and new flexibilities, it didn't engage my body and my sense of wonder, of mystery.

"What happens when our institutions no longer serve us, no longer reflect the truth of our own experience? We sit on pews and feel a soul-stirring discontent as we are preached sermons spoken from the dead. What we know is not what we hear," writes Terry Tempest Williams in her book *Leap*.

My mother always went to church, we all did, led by my father's insistence. He was a true believer. My mother dressed the part, taught Sunday school, but she never let me know if that hour or two in church had any relation at all to her life. Sometimes, listening to a particularly dull sermon—sincere but completely irrelevant to our lives—my mother would get a case of the giggles. We would join her in painfully suppressed laughter, shoulders shaking, avoiding one another's eyes, our faces reddening with the effort of controlling ourselves. My father would remain apart, holding on to the family dignity. I really don't think the church offered my mother any relevance or comfort, at least not its teachings as interpreted by our well-meaning but unimaginative male preachers. I can't believe that that mythology was something she felt in her bones, that held her up. What did sustain my mother was her commitment to the family she had made, to the perimeter formed by the six of us. The church and its teachings were not woven into the fabric of our daily lives, except that we were taught and led through bedtime prayers and, on special occasions, grace was recited at the dining room table.

✢

What I loved about church were the familiar hymns, no matter the words; the celebration of the turning of the year, especially Christmas; and the commitment to social action. But beyond the teachings of kindness and generosity that are at the basis of most any religion, I could not ask my child (or tell him) to memorize as truth the things that I had been taught. I found that I myself could still recite a few things that I memorized as a child, such as the Apostles' Creed, but I could not go phrase by phrase and tell my son, as I was taught in Sunday school, that this is what I believe, what I know to be true.

"I believe in God the Father Almighty, Maker of Heaven and Earth, and in Jesus Christ his only son, who was born of the virgin Mary, suffered under Pontius Pilate, was crucified, dead and buried. On the third day he rose again from the dead, where he sitteth on the right hand of God the Father Almighty. I believe in the Holy Ghost, the Holy Catholic Church, the forgiveness of sins, the resurrection of the body and life everlasting. Amen."

When I read this credo that is the basis of my religious instruction, certain words carry great weight and solemnity, and I fashion my own sort of creed:

"I believe in Earth. I want to believe in gods and goddesses. I know the suffering of mothers like Mary. I believe in roses, and the body, and the ascending blue heavens. I believe in sons and daughters and fathers. Forgiveness would be good. Amen."

Months after my trip to Fisheating Creek, at the gracious invitation of Dr. Bill Marquardt, an archaeologist with an abiding interest in the pre-Columbian Indians of south Florida, I visited what remains of the Fort Center mortuary carvings. The light was dim in the special collections storeroom of the Florida Museum of Natural History in Gainesville. Cradling the big eagle in gloved hands, I was surprised at the heartwood weight of it. The three-and-a-half-foot effigy carving sleeps or preens. Graceful curves of sinewy wood and empty ovals of space define the hunched power of its wing. Its head is turned left and down, the dark chestnut grain of the resting beak flowing into shoulder. All this from the core of one pine tree, carved with an adze made of conch shell, sanded with sharkskin and teeth. It could be kite. It could be eagle. It emanated solidity, an old power, perhaps, but no information, no sign or message that I could carry away with me. Regretfully, I returned the effigy to its resting spot on a shelf in the air-conditioned basement vault of the museum, where it will continue what vigil it can.

Through my own body, I have begun to teach myself to pray. It always starts with me pleading to the birds, the kites.

"People in the West are just beginning to retrieve ritual from the pits of their ancestral consciousness," writes African teacher Malidoma Some. "Ritual is called for because our soul communicates things to us that the body translates as need, or want, or absence. We enter into ritual in order to respond to the call of the soul."

I stand in a river, or the center of my garden, feeling myself extended between earth and sky. Standing, stretching, spine straight, feet dug into the cool river bottom or wiggled into ground. Feeling my own breathing, my own living body. Feeling the vibrations my physical body can channel. Knowing, noticing where I am. Where is north? East? South? West? Where are we in the turn of the year? How many days until the next solstice, equinox, quarter day? Where is the moon in its cycle? What are the names of the calling birds within my earshot? What am I grateful for? I connect with the blessing of simply being. I remember. This is how I pray.

For years, at every river crossing, I made this my practice— I stand barefoot in the tannic currents: "Bless me into usefulness. May I be of service to this beautiful planet. Keep my loved ones safe. Bless me onto my own true path. Bless me into serving kites."

And one day, standing just so in the Suwannee River at Fanning Springs, I remember who taught me to pray like this.

It was urgent, wild, undiscussed, expected.

"Who will be the first to see the ocean?" my mother would challenge, as we rounded south off the bridge between Kill Devil Hills and the mainland. "Who sees the lighthouse?"

Look for the light, she'd urge. Tell me when you catch sight of the sea.

And then, when we finally arrived, we'd tumble from the car, and we would run, no race, to touch the lip of the water, to gasp as the cold surf foam surged around our ankles and calves. She was teaching us body blessing water, water blessing body.

And when our time at the ocean was over, we would always be reminded by our mother to say goodbye to the ocean. To squat, to lean over the wet sand in our dry traveling clothes, to touch our fingers to the salt water. Unnamed gesture toward prayer.

"Goodbye, ocean! We'll be back," she'd have us chant.

"There are hundreds of ways to kneel and kiss the ground," said the poet Rumi.

Restorying

Once upon a time there must have been stories that people passed among themselves about swallow-tailed kites: they're far too dramatic to ignore. But in all my research, I haven't found even the barest fragments of a tale to explain what the convergence of the kite and the human has signified. Where is the poetry, where is the record, where are the words of context and wisdom? Where are the old stories? That's what I want to know.

In Florida, our population of sixteen million is remarkably transient and overwhelmingly unfamiliar with our natural land-scapes. Al Burt has written eloquently about the "absentee hearts" of many Floridians, whose bodies and winter homes are currently lodged in our state but whose loyalties and hearts reside elsewhere. It has not always been so. Most likely, the root of our inability to imagine and create a hopeful, inclusive vision for Florida lies in the waves of European conquistadors who invaded Florida between 1500 and 1800 A.D., exterminating or driving out all its native inhabitants. With the genocide of the original peoples, we lost a profound opportunity to understand our landscape.

Embedded in the old stories that sprang from intimate con-tact with living land was an ancient knowledge of how animals, including the human animal, can interact and cooperate with one another in a lasting fashion. This is where story matters. This is where the transmission from elder to child, aunt to niece, mother to son, is essential. This is, in fact, what we have lost in Florida. We have lost twelve thousand years of story in this land, story that once made sense of the landscape, how it grows, what it supports, how we must live. This loss extends beyond Florida, to the continent of North America itself as inhabited by the colonizing peoples.

What does it mean to live on unstoried land? How does such poverty of heritage relate to attachment and stewardship of a landscape? Without stories, without specifying the sacred, we can hold nothing holy, nothing whole. We desecrate because "we know not what we do." Nor where we really are, nor what makes this place work.

From a seventh-floor hotel room, released from a day of business meetings, I watched the ocean nibble the edge of Florida's northernmost sea island—Amelia. Standing before the plate glass window, I yanked my bathing suit up over my body, anxious to be outside in the last of the light. Even as I raced down to the beach, my thoughts were taken up with swallow-tailed kites. I wouldn't see them here, I knew that; they were far away to the south and west, in the peninsula's interior, this late in the summer.

I strode the beach fast, watching streamers of terns slip down the wind to their night roost on Ward's Bank, grateful to be moving along the wild edge of the Atlantic. By matching my ears against the high sea wind's roar, until sound balanced between them, I could tell that my body was headed due south, directly into the source of the powerful air. Brown pelicans, wingtip to water, soothed the sea into inky black rest.

I half-jogged, half-walked the beach until past dark, deep in thought. I wondered whether, despite our impoverished cultural legacy in Florida today, there wasn't a path that might return me to the true ways of this land. I remembered the words of Chickasaw poet Linda Hogan: "The landscape itself, despite its tragic losses, remains storied."

So before I returned to the great lit hotel, I stood in the sea, asking the planet to tell me a story, some piece of the sacred collective memory—that regarding the swallow-tailed kite—driven into the air when the Europeans annihilated the native peoples of Florida. I prayed hard.

Back in the hotel room, my body tingled, wild with attending to the night. I felt too big now, too rangy for the confines of the small unfamiliar space. Pacing back and forth around the bed, I felt ready to explode with a primitive, physical longing. It didn't feel like giving birth—more like coupling, like making the baby, like making the story. My hair was thickened with salt wind, the caverns of my body slippery and fertile. It wasn't a human lover I craved, although I was aching to merge. What kind of tale might be told about kites to explain their mystery and appeal? I thought of the range maps of birds I have studied, the webbing of migratory paths connecting continents from the north to the south, and began to piece together a sort of origin moment for the birds I loved. I attended to my prayer and my question, dropped into meditation like a skimmer falling into the sea wind. Images came to me, of the restless planet long, long ago, full of hot lava and great heat. I imagined watching the earth spin from space, how the oceans teetered up against the edges of the land, sloshing. I pictured the continents jostling one another, how underneath the mild surface, great tectonic plates, the uncertain bones of the earth, fought for position and space. I imagined a creation myth that might explain the roles of the living animals, how they would join with gravity to keep the planet from simply flying apart.

What if the Creator had actually assigned each species a role (which indeed they do have)? The bison and the elk and the deer would hold the grasses and the soil with their hooves; the pelicans would quiet the sea waves with their widespread, low-riding wings. The smaller birds might be given the job of tying together the Northern Hemisphere and the Southern: the phalarope and the least tern, the dowitcher and the spotted sandpiper, the vermilion flycatcher and the painted bunting. Perhaps the swallow-tailed kite, living in the great open prairie lands of Brazil, would have been designated one of the first birds to fly north because of its powerful ability to glide. Maybe it looked more ordinary than it does today. Perhaps once upon a time its tail was no longer nor more remarkable than a hawk's, except, of course, for the bobbin of sticky, invisible thread the Creator had hidden under its tail feathers. And maybe, before it began the long flight to Florida, she also buried a tiny chip of lime rock near its heart, as a sort of compass to guide the bird north to its assigned place. And so the kite would have flown north over the high Andes, up the neck of Central America, and over to Cuba on its way to our continent. As the bird began the last long leg of its journey, over the Gulf of Mexico, it might have encountered one of the powerful cold fronts that sweeps across the continent each winter, wave after wave of wind, and it had to fight and strain to stay on course to Florida. The pull of the thread on its tail must have been strong, but still the bird beat on to our peninsula, bent on connecting it to the south. So that by the time the bird dropped exhausted into the piney woods of the Big Cypress, in south Florida, its tail had been drawn and split into a long scissortail—but the threads binding the continents were intact.

In this story, we can imagine how the kite became swallow-tailed and how it participates to this day with the other migratory species in a great weaving of the planet whole, a crisscrossing of invisible threads, bringing just the necessary tension from South America to the Yukon. In this way, the animals offer us reassurance against the uncertain volcanoes, the precarious tectonic plates, and the restless planet's spinning. Unaccountably reassured, I finally drifted to sleep, thinking of the kite and its place in the world.

Some months later, I began to wonder: What are the larger myths or stories that I hold in common with my fellow North Americans, or with people born into the middle class in New Jersey, or with transplanted Floridians? What tales were told to us that inform our life choices?

As far as I can remember, neither of my parents "told stories," though my father read to my sister and me every single night when we were small. They only spoke about our forebears if we really pressed. And even then, the stories were thin, only tangentially related to our own lives.

My mother didn't tell stories at all, although she loved to sum up a situation with a proverb, such as "A new broom sweeps clean" or "You can't teach an old dog new tricks." It was always understood to be a bit of a joke: the telling was intended for our amusement—we could laugh and be delighted that we had found a circumstance to match with a saying. As if it were humorous somehow, that something that occurred in real life could be informed by folk wisdom. This habit offered us camaraderie. And the real fit was that we could all laugh together; the common thread was our agreement that this was a funny thing. Our myth was the absence of real myth.

Coming from such a family is like trying to understand the configuration of life under the living sea by walking along the shoreline, examining the sea wrack at the high-tide line. Each of those tiny angelwing shells was once joined to another, a twin, and together they enclosed the life of a single creature, like a single day in the life of someone who bore me. All I can do is guess what their lives were like, just as I can only guess, not visualize, the living time of the cleanly blank seashells along the shore. Did they live close to shore or far out in the gulf? Under the sandy bottom or in and among a reef of some sort? I may be able to dig out some facts from a science text, but as far as the living flesh of the mollusk, or the emotional life of my elders, that's gone. Fragments are all I have. I long for women who might have sat with me around an unsteady kitchen table, chopping peppers and onions, telling me who I am, where I come from, unraveling what I am here to do.

If we believe we have no satisfactory stories handed down from our own blood people, then what can we tell our children? When David was small, just finding his way into language, he wanted us to tell him stories, as all young ones do. Like my own parents, I read to him for hours at a time, although

I rarely spun tales of my own. My husband, on the other hand, could always come up with a story. Sometimes I stood just beyond David's bedroom door, as transfixed as our boy by his father's made-up stories, such as this:

> David, one day, you and your big green [imaginary] parrot named Mr. Smith were out in the woods behind our house, working on our trails. I [Daddy] was at work. You were using our pruning clippers to cut back the thorny greenbrier vines that always grow over our paths, and Mr. Smith was flying around from branch to branch, keeping you company. All of a sudden, you found yourself caught in a sticker vine, and then another, and another, until you were trapped and couldn't move! Mr. Smith saw the bad situation and flew all the way to my office, flapping and flapping, down Yashuntafun Road, turning right at the corner, flying over all the cars on Apalachee Parkway, all the way to downtown Tallahassee. He came straight to my office and pecked on my window. Peck, peck, peck. I knew that you must need help, so I put Mr. Smith in my car and drove all the way home, fast, and got a really big pair of clippers and cut you free, and we all had a party to celebrate the clever Mr. Smith.

How did he come up with that, I marveled, watching the small body of my son settle into his father's arms in the soft round chair? I don't think he consciously planned how to weave in the messages the boy needed to hear, of magic birds, adventure, humor, a visual map of where the family lived and worked, and the assurance that, even while far away, the father was connected to the child and would always be available to him if he needed help. But that is what he did.

We live forward from the stories embedded within us, whether we agreed to hear them or not. Whether we knew they were being told or not.

I see now that what my parents and aunts and uncles and

grandparents were telling us, unconsciously embedding in us, were not so much stories as dreams. Thinking back, I can see how dreams, like good stories, get told despite themselves, when the teller taps into those things that keep him or her alive with possibility. You can recognize a story (or a dream) being told by the teller's shift into a new voice, out of dailiness and household preoccupations. In my childhood, my parents' excited stories were almost always about the future: the places we might travel to (and did); the new house we could have built in the new town my father's company transferred us to (we did); the beach property we might finally save enough to buy (and did); the campground in south Jersey we could buy and how we could drop right out of the "rat race" and manage it ourselves (we didn't). These were dream-stories common to our time, stories of people who had inherited both hunger and the desire to create security from their immigrant forebears, just after the Depression and two world wars. They were the stories of people who believed in the American Dream. When we visited the General Electric exhibit at the 1965 World's Fair in New York City, we heard a powerful story regarding the possibilities of future inventions. The promises of that exhibit inducted us into our present consumer culture, which forty years later stupefies us with choice and excess.

My own history is lost to me, yet I am still acting from it, unconscious. Given that I actually was imbued with my parents' dreams, stories of a kind, what is it that I'm saying I knew so little about?

The story I did not get, none of us got, is a tale of ourselves in reciprocal, sustainable relationship with this North American continent (or any other landscape). My people emerged one hundred years ago from cold northern European landscapes, rocky, with long winters, and whatever their stories, they must not have encouraged or lent hope or light because my people, in my memory, are largely mute. We were among those living out the perception of a great exodus from Europe, looking for the promised land. We share stories with our whole culture, of pushing back the frontier, of surviving or succumbing to great hardship and threat. We have been told the story of ourselves overcoming the adversarial forces of nature and native peoples, those who resisted our terrible advance over the continent. Instead of stories of tribal identity in particular places, we honor pioneer stories, all about transience, in which the protagonists continually move on, romantically alone in wilderness, repeatedly reinventing home, with a thinly rooted sense of place at best.

Our immigrant forebears viewed this continent as a place to transcend and were incapable of allowing themselves to be touched by the continent as a presence of the divine. "As now constituted, North American culture has no story of its origin in Nature, and rampages across the planet," writes Bruce Wilshire in his book *Wild Hunger*. Affixed as we are in small, nuclear family dramas, stories not going back very far, we cannot place ourselves in the broad movement to this continent; nor have we identified the truth of what our lifestream has done and is doing to life already here. And so maybe it isn't really a single family myth I am longing for but a way of being.

A woman called my home on an April night. She wanted to talk to me about swallow-tailed kites. She spoke with an intensity that matched my own. I didn't know her at all. She had been told to call me by a close mutual friend. She wanted to help me with this kite story and wondered: What could she do?

I'd been preoccupied, not thinking as much about kites. In her urgency, she required me to think again about my questions.

"There should be a story about kites," I said. "But I haven't found anything, and since all pre-European settlement history has been erased, I probably never will. That's why I've made up my own."

"Oh, but there are stories about kites," she said. "They are the spiritual center, they are everything's context for a Venezuelan people and other South American people as well."

I gripped tight to the telephone, hardly believing what I heard. "Oh, please, can you tell me everything you know about this?" I begged.

The next evening, Karla Brandt stopped by my house, bringing me several papers about shamanism as practiced in the present day by the Matsigenka people, who live in the rain forests between the upper Manu and the upper Madre de Dios rivers in Peru.

Karla sat across my kitchen table, accepted a cup of tea. "These people practice a rich and complex religious tradition, full of metaphor, which is tightly bound to the plants and animals of the region," she said. "And the most important guardian spirit of the Matsigenka is the *matsi'panko*, in our language, the swallow-tailed kite. The shamans say the actual birds, kites encountered by the people in their daily lives, are not spirits; rather, they are considered the 'grandchildren' of the *matsi'panko* spirit."

Late into the night, I studied Karla's gifts. In one book, an anthology entitled *Portals of Power*, published by the University of New Mexico Press, there was an excerpt from the song of the guardian spirit *matsi'panko*: "I am flying, I have come flying, over hills. . . . I turn round myself as I fly. Have you seen my grandchildren, whose caps are white?"

The researcher Gerhard Baer writes that the shamans of this culture, assisted by their guardian and auxiliary spirits, perform many essential roles, including mediation, clairvoyance, protection from dangerous illnesses and hunger, and the example of living a ritually pure life.

And it's not just this one tribe that draws on the kite for ritual.

"The relation between the shaman and the swallow-tailed

Our True Home

When my son entered kindergarten, I returned to full-time work at the state wildlife agency, settling on an early schedule to stagger child-care duties with my husband. He would get our son off to school, and I would pick him up at 4:30 p.m.

Weekday mornings, I rose and dressed before daylight, brushed my child's hair from his forehead as he stirred to wake, knowing that was all that I would have of him, and give to him, until the end of our respective days at school and work. Then I'd run downstairs and back the car out of the driveway, headlights catching snapshots of our garden—the first blooms of my favorite antique rose or the pumpkin yellow cosmos at the edge of the woods. The rising sun would be reflecting in the windows of the big building where I worked when I wheeled into the empty parking lot: few of my co-workers chose to begin so early. On the windowless walls of my office, I tacked dozens of images of things I loved, the Suwannee River, swallow-tailed kites, cabbage palms, my family.

"Maybe you can reframe your work space as a cave," my friend Norine suggested. "Is there any way to think of it as cozy?"

But on the below-ground floor, my co-workers and I felt not only the absence of light but also the weight of the multiple stories of the building above. We medicated ourselves with chocolate and sweet lemonade and expensive coffee and with the promise of going out to lunch. Sometimes we'd hear a rumble and wonder if a thunderstorm was happening outside or if it was simply people moving their heavy furniture around on the floors above us. Restricted to chair and computer, I watched my body thicken and grow soft. I developed repetitive strain injuries from too much keyboarding. When new people came on, kite is widely distributed across South America, from Guiana, the Orinoco delta and the Apapocuva-Guarani in the east, to the Tunebo, the Desana, and the Matsigenka in the west," Baer summarizes. "For the Apapocuva-Guarani, swallow-tailed kites are closely associated with thunderstorms and rain, and thus fertility of plants. The kites' tail feathers are used as a center-piece on ceremonial diadems worn by tribal shamans."

I'd always thought the bird must mean that much to some peoples; now I know it. I am stunned by the chasm between ourselves, worshiping distant gods indoors, and indigenous peoples, invoking and protecting the very creatures that share their space.

used to a more physical life, like my friend Lora, at first they'd resist the sedentary nature of our jobs. Lora set her watch timer, and every fifty minutes, I could hear her drop to the floor: thirty push-ups, she told me, on the hour.

When I'd brought my son to the office, he was bewildered by my job. "Mom, I don't know what you, or Dad, or Uncle Jon do for a living. Everyone just seems to sit in offices and talk on the phone, or answer e-mail. . . . What do any of you actually do?"

It wasn't only my child that I missed. It was movement. Light. Air. And I no longer saw kites. They are late risers and do not coast into the sky until hours after I began work in my windowless office. I remembered that slower time, a schedule of home tending and writing and volunteering in my son's class-room. Of course I didn't make much money, and of course I lived an easy version of normal life, compared with most people. But what I was doing now was not the life my animal body desired.

I began to set the clock for 5:15 a.m. and rose quietly, wrapping myself in a quilt on the rocker on my back porch, listening and looking at the day beginning, writing by the light of a single candle. I would push the page of my notebook close to that tiny light, sometimes moving my pen without being able to see the marks it made.

The first sign of night giving way, of there being more than what the moon provided, was the shout of the cardinal, his flame of a body pulled taut as a bowstring as he delivered his song. Even in the dark, I knew this—I had seen it so many times in the light of day. He seemed to claim, through only voice, the bounds of his nesting place.

After a time I picked out the outline of a familiar hickory, just its profile, and then the ground resumed its form. I could see that all the shadows mattered—every shadow matters. With the first faint wash of blue to the sky, a barred owl called the change. The crows woke, creaking into their speech, and then the first parula warbler and a Carolina wren. The eastern sky thickened like a pudding on the stovetop, pooling with color where the sun would soon appear.

The swamp rose swam into view through the screen of the porch, and I smelled its perfume, suddenly let down with the light. A warm summery mist, the breath of the trees, muffled the woods. I inhaled that real air and its particular burden of moisture and pollen, its wanderings, its holding of the birds. This was not trapped, recirculated air, artificially heated or cooled. Moments before, these very molecules had slid across the surface of oak leaves and through the feathers of woodpeckers. These woodpeckers, my neighbors: if I didn't take time with them, we'd become strangers. I'd no longer know which of the trees they were listening to, probing, hammering, healing.

I never saw the kites at this time of the day; it was still too early for them to be up and about. I guessed what they were doing: perched in small, silent family groups in the dark. To fly in the heavy morning air, a kite would have to flap heavily, use too much energy. Instead, perhaps they were beginning to preen, running bills through feathers, restoring the precise gaps where yesterday's electric air pushed aside structure. Tending each feather in turn, caring for those thermal-climbing tools. I knew that, like me, they listened to the absorption of the cardinal with its own voice, calling the limits of territory.

One April day, about eight months after I returned to full-time indoor work, I had a chance to visit the Bull Creek Wildlife Management Area south of Orlando to research a travel story. As usual, I hoped I'd see kites. I spent the necessary hours in the thinly treed uplands, reworking an interpretive brochure but always keeping an eye on the horizon where cypress domes rose and fell like soft emerald hills, breathing. The summertime habitat of the swallow-tailed kite.

It's rarely a quick business, finding these birds. But I went looking for them down in that creek bottom after my work was done. Yellow-throated vireos called all around me, their songs mingling with the shouts of a pair of red-shouldered hawks. Pineapple-like bromeliads sprang stiff and delicate from most all the trees, some with gaudy red flowering stalks. A hummingbird moved through the woods, noisy in its own small way. From the floodplain forest, two turkey hunters emerged, dressed in camouflage and knee-high rubber boots, making their way out of the swamp.

"Any luck?" I asked the hunters.

"Just a few hens walking around," one replied.

"Seen any swallow-tailed kites?" I asked in my particular language of what luck looks like.

"Sure, maybe thirty this season on the Wildlife Management Area, up by our hunt camp on Crabgrass Creek, here at the Ford, and two last Saturday at Billy Lake."

Envy flooded me. From the hunters' accounting, I gathered that as many as a half a dozen pairs of kites were nesting nearby. I wanted to intersect with their living, but I was down for only the day, flying into Orlando early, driving here, flying out at dark. The hunters, on the other hand, had risen at 3:30 a.m. at their camp just a couple of miles from this creek. Long before dawn, they unloaded a small boat, forded the creek, followed their flagging tape by flashlight to a scouted site, and waited. They waited for six or seven hours. And they do that day after day. They don't just drop out of the sky in a plane, get in a rental car, and pull up in what looks like good turkey swamp and expect to shoot one. They scout and wait and sit and walk and call and plan. I spend most of my days in an office, but always I long for kites and the fully sensate life they represent to me.

As I prepared to head to my own home, standing at the creek's edge, watching the water's surface teem with thousands of minute, emerging insects, I reminded myself: it's not a quick business, this being with wild things, whether we wish to hunt them or merely watch. We need a slower time.

We must take in and name as much as we are able of the natural world, our true home. It's an immediate sort of skill—this knowing of our habitat—one that used to mean the difference between our lives and our deaths. It cannot be acquired through television or computer or from inside buildings at all. We can't do much of it looking through a car window, and none at all in a mall. We are real animals, gone far too deeply into our heads and the abstract end of the continuum of all we are capable of as humans. Because we spend so much time in "virtual reality," we lose the daily practice with what is real, and our bodies and our senses grow slack. Still, our technological visions allude to our lost world, present enough hints of our broken contact, our loss of wholeness, our loss of animal immersion in the habitat that is our birthright, that we feel loss.

A day doesn't go by that I don't talk about kites to someone, think about them. In the course of moving so quickly from errand to errand in my car, so preoccupied, I still look at what bits of the sky I can, knowing I'm not likely to see them downtown where I work but not wanting to miss an opportunity to see them pass over high, on some swift errand that doesn't involve the city.

Sometimes, at the end of the workday, after dinner and a bit of family time, I slip out the side door to walk down our red clay road at dusk. Even though I'm returned to the real world, after sitting all day working with my head, it's hard to shrug the habit of thinking, to simply walk and watch. Over and over, my eyes are drawn down to the ground and back into my head, instead of really registering the movement of the trees or the speed and shift of the clouds. If it wasn't for the buzzing in my brain—mind talk, chatter, self-absorption, doubt, question, classification, dissection, worry—that constant and uninvited but oh so familiar brain buzz, what might my moving through space be like? What if for a whole two-mile walk my skin was in charge, just my skin, no words, simply sensation of cold, light, leaf shade, breeze, insect sting, whatever comes? A vocabulary of skin might rival the English language if only I could put a hand over the brain chatter, a gentle, firm quieting, a dark washcloth, perhaps, so that if it just couldn't stop talking, at least its words would be muffled into the damp, thick navy-blue terrycloth, and I would be free to listen to the world with my skin. Or ears—how about ears? What if I could really register every sound, not only the brown thrasher, the red-bellied woodpecker, but the meaning of bird? And the brush of leaf against leaf, and the sibilance of oak snake through sheep sorrel, and the creep of the wind through the stamens of the coral honeysuckle. And then I would have to give equal time to my nose, to the last airborne bits of the yellow fragrance of the jessamine and all the scents of the evening that I just missed because of the dominance of the thinking part of my being. The fragrance of courting pileated woodpeckers.

And more about skin: feeling the full extent of the cold well water, for instance, the lime rock– derived water pulled from the dark river under this land sprinkled through my fingers to snug down the dirt around my peas, those little satisfying spikes of emerald. If I had felt that water running from the hose through my fingers onto those peas even more intimately, then I would see that it doesn't matter if I planted them too late; what matters is that moment of feeling the water, seeing the green, smelling their marriage, being here, making more space to be here and to get the brain talk to quiet. My brain, the baby child of my body-mind-spirit, spoiled like our youngest kitten, believing it is all there is and using up so much living whining and worrying when the skin, and the ear, and the nose, and the mouth each have a language.

After about a mile of walking fast, I am fully returned to the present. I am again my animal body, moving at a brisk clip over the crisp clay road, much more alert than when I began. I stop for a few minutes to lie belly down on the dry soil, my face turned to the side, feeling how quickly my life pulses against the slow, deep ground. So much movement in me now, so rapid, so fluttery, like the movement of moth wings flailing at glass, so quick like the heartbeat of a rabbit imprisoned in your hands or even in its own fearful body.

It was still early enough in the evening, so I gathered my son, my niece, and my nephew, and we walked a long time toward sunset. Under the wide sky, red bellies of storm clouds washed the clay surface of the road, the children, and the rain puddles into all one pink, all one joyfulness. David ran to me, offering a feathery globe of dandelion flower. I blew and blew the winged seeds, asking fiercely of each wild weedlet that it grow me into more passionate, intimate living.

Call and Response

Words are what I do for a living, but I do not trust them entirely. They do not generally sink to the bone. They can be retracted. In my job at the state wildlife conservation agency, I sometimes witnessed the rewriting of truth by editing or by excision. Example: I was assigned to write a five-hundred-word piece on the natural history of the whooping crane for a Florida lifestyle magazine. I listed the things that have led to the bird's extreme endangerment, and one of these threats was hunting. Deliberate shooting. Hot bullets hurtling into flesh and feathers. I didn't put it that graphically, of course. I simply wrote: "Habitat loss and illegal hunting were among the causes of this crane's decline."

A supervisor one hopscotch above me in the agency chain of command handed me back the story draft: "Take out the part about hunting," he said.

"Why?" I asked, horrified. "That's what happened! It was true!"

"It will just upset our constituents," he said. "We don't need to go there. It doesn't happen anymore."

Before he would allow the story to go forward, he required me to backspace that phrase, those true words, right off the page. As if it never happened. In this way, we rewrote history, made it prettier and more palatable, just a little bit of it, just a little at a time. And supposedly that was okay because our agency is the powerful ally of wildlife, its primary advocate in our state, the place where the best resources are centered.

But it makes me wonder, What else has not been said?

What if you are only told part of the truth? What if I know something essential and I withhold it from you because it is so painful?

⚜

Sometimes scientists are fabulous storytellers; Ken Meyer is one of them. I've wondered: If these experts are willing to tell all they know, as Ken does, aren't their words enough to see to the planet's conservation, and swallow-tailed kites specifically? The biologists I know are articulate and airtight and can be passionate, even, as they report their findings. And since they are the experts, what is my role? Especially if I am not willing to restrict myself to merely reporting what others have learned? I suspect there is more to the truth, to world-changing truth telling, than the unadorned facts of science, important as they are.

About eight years ago, I was invited along with twenty-five other environmentalists to meet with Florida's lieutenant governor in rare, intimate conversation. We gathered in a circle in the plush living room of a remote ranch house near Ocala, speaking in turn on behalf of our organizations: Sierra, Audubon, Friends of the Everglades, the Nature Conservancy, 1000 Friends of Florida, others. My colleagues asked the lieutenant governor to speed the Everglades cleanup, fund more land acquisition, do more for energy conservation. Everyone was eloquent, full of facts, advocating like the lawyers many of them were. My turn drew closer; I didn't have any planned remarks. My heart raced; I felt myself shivering. All I could think about were kites.

And so I launched into an unrehearsed description of the plight of swallow-tailed kites in Florida. I described the vulnerable roost, the graceful birds, my desire for my young son to be able to see them all his life, and for all Florida's children to know and revere them. My eyes shone with hot tears. I had no hard data or solutions to offer. My throat closed; I stopped. The lieutenant governor responded to me, kindly, vaguely. No one else spoke. The woman next to me picked up with the Everglades legal suit as if I had never spoken. I averted my gaze, hugged my knees, felt a fool. I had violated an unspoken rule of this political setting. I had exposed my heart.

I gazed out the plate-glass windows, wondering if I would ever be an effective advocate if I couldn't keep my emotions under wraps. Or if I'd ever want to. As I sagged into the misery of my thoughts, a swallow-tailed kite arced into view, alive, glinting white against the blue sky, just outside the window glass. It shouldn't be here now, I thought to myself. The others of its kind are all at the Okeechobee roost, readying to set out across the gulf for South America.

I caught the eye of a friend; he winked, smiled. I settled back into my body. The others talked on.

The writer Muriel Rukeyser describes two kinds of poetry: the poetry of "unverifiable fact"—that which emerges from dreams, sexuality, subjectivity; and the poetry of "documentary fact"—literally, accounts of strikes, wars, geographical and geological details, actions of actual persons in history, scientific invention. Our culture is most comfortable with documentary fact, the truth of the scientists and academics. What I notice is how split apart are these two ways of knowing truth. One embodied. The other, generally not.

By paying attention to my body, I am learning to feel my way into truth. Just as the rivers are truths carved into the body of the planet, undeniable channels, so we may allow ourselves to fall into the larger body of the earth, rather than the surficial currents and tinny voices of the dominant culture. In the river, the water is tannic and dark, and we cannot see our way to the bottom. We may collide with hard cypress knees or scrape our feet on the lime rock bottom, which is bedrock, what we seek.

One time a swallow-tailed kite, strung taut on its light bones, swooped above me, a pair of kingbirds in close chase. The kite powered fast into the canopy of a spreading live oak, but not before I glimpsed the nestling gripped in its talons. I had forgotten that side of my long-winged birds, how they rip young birds from their nests and eat them raw, floating on the slight breath of the wind.

I organized an expedition to Tall Timbers Research Station about thirty miles north to look for yellow-breasted chats with my friend, ornithologist Todd Engstrom. The trip was a birthday present for another bird-loving nephew, Garrett, who, with my son, David, hoped to add this secretive warbler to his life list of birds. As we moved slowly through the old pines, easing toward the brushy habitat preferred by chats, Todd quizzed us, tuning up our ears—the voices of birds coupled with a practiced ear are generally the best tools for identifying them in the field. All around us birdsong poured down from the sky.

"Parula warbler," we named. "And pine warbler, great crested flycatcher, red-bellied woodpecker. Northern bob-white."

"What about that one?" he asked, gesturing toward a two-phrased singing.

"Yellow-throated vireo," said my nephew Garrett, quickly, while my own brain shuffled through image and song more slowly.

"Good," said Todd, nodding.

We climbed out of the truck, and where Todd stood became the center, as if at the heart of a compass, his arms the connections between hidden bird and human knowing. He stood at the heart of all that a lifetime of paying close attention in the woods had brought him, the knowledge of each avian voice, without hesitation.

"Indigo bunting." Right arm toward the west, paired notes, long phrasing. "Blue grosbeak."

A slurred *pee-a-weee*: "Eastern wood-pewee."

"Ground dove." Different from the common mourning dove, a single, distinct *coo*.

Each song I have learned before. Some I hear only once a year, some daily. The neurons linking memory and name fire quickly or slowly, depending on intimacy, mine, with each bird's call.

"Yellow-breasted chat!" Todd signaled. There it was, and the boys were happy, plunging off into the brush to see the bird, for that is how they love to keep their lists. For them, the sighting means almost everything; for me it is habitat and voice.

"Orchard oriole," says Todd, arm directed high, east. I do not even pick out the notes from the rest at all.

"Where, where?" I ask, frantic to keep up.

We wait, listening.

There, he says again, chopping his extended arm more precisely in the direction of the bird's singing.

I'm frustrated at how barely the oriole's song registers in my brain. It's a different kind of not hearing. I am willing, even eager, to hear the bird and memorize its notes so I'll know in the future when I'm near it, but I am so unpracticed with its sound.

Do you see the danger of this kind of ignorance? If I cannot hear the bird and don't see it, it doesn't exist. Nor might its precise habitat, the things it requires to live. The bird must sing. We must hear it call. Then we must be able to name the animal and what it needs. Then it is time for our voices. Our responding. Our protection of these lives.

The call notes of the birds and their songs go out into the silence, and on the other side of their rattle or scream or song is the same absence of sound. But is it really the same? Is anything changed for the sounding? Do the actual waves of sound that reach my eardrums change anything in any way? Probably birdsong often does induce or suggest movement by others of their kind: I am here. I am foraging. I am looking for a mate. I am a good provider. I have an excellent nest site. There is a predator nearby. I am alive, I am here, I exist. In the swamp forest among the lifting trunks of trees, under the gray sky, the landscape shivers with the circling call of the red-shouldered hawk. Perhaps in some way the rolling waves of sound of the wild things move against one another physically, even at some level contributing to the upholding of trunks, the stance of tall grasses, a counteractive force against gravity. Perhaps voice is a physical part of the matrix of things.

The loss of each species, the muting of any one voice, creates a hole in infinity, limits earth's possibilities. The point of speaking about truth is this: we have a real world, and too much of it is really dying. One of the most captivating aspects of the history of the European settlement of North America is the establishment of democracy, implying a voice for all, as well as a broader tolerance than the monarchies across the Atlantic allowed. But in fact there was a much broader pluralism on this continent before colonization.

We have had to order our lives around denial of this truth, or we couldn't go on in our daily lives as we do. Thirty thousand species, thirty thousand different kinds of lives and voices are wiped from the planet by our excesses and ignorance each year. By our belief that our needs and hungers are greater than the rest of the planet.

But we are also acquainted with the power of voice for the good: how Rachel Carson chose to use that sense of hearing in titling her book *Silent Spring*, thus alerting us to the terrible legacy of pesticides in the 1960s. It's clear that those of us who can raise our heads above denial, and the diversions of the popular culture and our own hopelessness, need to use every variation on voice we have at our disposal to bring the rest of us along: describe and alert and growl and chant and pray. Croon and whisper and extol and harmonize. Adore and alarm and mourn and insist.

Level of the Land

It's been ten years since I began to travel intentionally after swallow-tailed kites. Even when I am not in their presence (most of the time now), what I have learned of their lives orients me in time and place. But the arc of kite country in southwest Florida that I learned from Ken Meyer pulls me still. When I drive through Labelle or Clewiston or the town of Okeechobee, I feel close to the center of kites, and I usually make time to linger. Early on an April morning, I found myself in just such a moment, driving east toward West Palm on Highway 80 from Ft. Myers. I took the familiar left-hand jog on U.S. 27 toward Moore Haven, marveling again at the uniform stands of grassy sugarcane that filled the flat basin of the land for miles on every side. Even though I knew the kites themselves wouldn't gather here in great numbers until at least July, I detoured in their direction.

As I passed the barbed wire enclosure of the Glades County Correctional Institution, I found myself listening to an interview of former attorney general Janet Reno. She was talking about the president's crime bill and about comprehensive prevention programs. How simply locking up the bad guys will not ultimately keep us safe. I could see how that was true for the kites, too, only in reverse. We can't confine them to big preserves to protect them: they won't have it. That's only where some of them live, and only for part of the year. They need the preserves, yes, but they also need Fisheating Creek to roost. They must have Lake Okeechobee and this entire southern landscape to forage; they require large expanses of Central and South American rain forest to overwinter and safe passage across the gulf in between.

I began traveling after kites with what I thought was a simple intent—to be close to a bird I had loved for twenty years. But the story that has unfolded goes beyond the natural history of the swallow-tailed kite: it is the natural history of us, in south Florida, us as North Americans in the early twenty-first century. The story penetrates how I perceive and satisfy my own needs. It includes the way I live my life, the size of my house, the food I eat, the things I buy, the way I travel. I chose kites, or they have chosen me, but I could have selected the monarch butterfly or the parula warbler or a Florida black bear or a Haitian sugarcane worker to serve this story. Each creature is linked to every other in the intricate web of life. The lives of the migrant workers who harvest the sugarcane outside my car window are just as degraded as are those of the kites who breathe the agricultural pesticides; as are the rivers and lakes that receive the cane's nitrogenous wastes; as are the teeth of our children and ourselves, who eat sixty-eight pounds of sugar each and every year; as are the souls of the rich few who get even richer off all the rest.

When I reached Nicodemus Slough, I parked my car on the left flank of the lake, ducked around the steel bar gate, and walked west on the Herbert Hoover Dike. Steady light breezes slid past my face; a sheeting cloud cover drew the sky up from the south. It was so good to get out of the car. The dike, an enormous trapezoid of dug earth, stood as high as a temple; it was built in the 1950s to corral the free-flowing waters of the greater Everglades, so wide that four semitrucks could drive side by side on its crunchy lime rock crown. Its long shoulders, clothed with closely mown bahia grass and an assortment of weeds, tapered gently to the true surface of the land. At the base of the dike to my left a broad brown canal abruptly edged with Brazilian pepper, cattail, willow, and palm knifed toward the lake. Beyond, a gaggle of prefab mobile homes trimmed with square collars of turf clung to the canal's edge as if it were true water.

To the south, past the cattle egrets and grackles strutting and picking through the sharp grasses on that inert edifice's slope, a lot more life was happening. A landscape of wet palm prairie, copses of spreading live oak, pocket wetlands edged with elderberry, pickerel weed, and cattail stretched to the spacious horizon, in the direction of my desire. Three sandhill cranes prodded in the mud, twitching aside roots; close by, great egrets and white ibis fished, each according to its individual fashion. A brown-feathered northern harrier, female, tilted over the marsh at waist height, and meadowlarks with their black-chevroned yellow chests filled up all the spaces with their singing.

I kicked up a pile of black feather and bone, remnants of a common moorhen, in the trail under my feet. I thought about the impartiality of wild landscapes, how the winds blow as easily through the grounded feathers of this eaten waterbird as they caress a live one cackling among the reeds. And how the weighting of the living biomass shifts: there's a more robust marsh hawk or eagle cleaning its bill on a snag somewhere close, one less moorhen gabbling amid its kind. The problem for our planet is not so much this sort of ancient give and take but the quantities of resources commandeered by our single species. I see how the land allows and allows, counting on us to devise and live by sustainable checks and balances. So far we have not.

A purple gallinule picked with her chick through the lily pads on the water's surface, reminding me of a similar pair of birds—red-necked grebes—I watched from the shore of Brown's Lake in western Montana last summer. It was the immature's incessant begging, repeatedly urging the parent down for more food, that first caught my attention. As large in body as the careworn parent, thick with its feedings, the young grebe waited for its parent to surface with food gleaned from the lake bottom. I thought to myself how like the stripe-headed young grebe we are as a society, resting on privilege, not yet evolved into self-nurturing adults. We struggle to quell our old wild hungers with material goods, asking more of the earth than it can sustainably provide, forcing thousands of species out of existence. We seem incapable of clear diving into dark water after our true needs: story, spirit, intimacy.

It matters that we know and name what we need, for otherwise, the forces of corporate economism package and advertise what they want us to desire, to buy. We become confused by the slick wrapping, bright lights, and intricate promises. And we come to believe that these excesses—the very things that are killing our planet—are exactly what we need, what we must have. Kites don't manufacture the threats to their existence. They have, can have, very little effect on the world we share with them. But we do. I wondered if pulling back from our out-of-control consumer culture might not be the most useful thing I could do to help the birds I love.

I thought about the roles other consumers—the animal predators—might play: What does the eagle offer to the moorhen in exchange for its life? There's this: the eagle takes exactly and only what it needs. And perhaps in the heart-banging chase and capture, it keeps the others knife-edge alert to the business of living. Maybe the eagle's gift to the moorhen is the culling of the weak or the slow so that the moorhen as a species can rise to its maximum efficiency. But we can't claim that is what we give the rest of the planet through our version of predation, our overconsumption.

I veered off the rocky track and slid down the rough grasses to the ground. I bent low to place my palms in the water, eye level with the true level of the land. Here I could sense the very tip of life dividing and multiplying into deliberate green form, or flesh, in the cranes, in the cypress, in the lily pads.

A thousand years ago, even three or four hundred, this would have been my place and my perspective. I would be peering up from some work, tending to a child or a row of squash plants—among the creatures, within the landscape, not above it. I might have squatted close to the ground as I am now, staring at the unsettled sky with its south-born clouds, taking in the insistent voice of the red-shouldered hawk, harassed and driven by a scattering of crows. I might have set down my digging stick, looking even higher at the vultures circling, with a cara-cara and an anhinga surprisingly mixed into their invisible cauldron of air current, and then at the pair of kites, suddenly appearing as they do, simply another miracle among the whole of community. The kites would not have had to carry so much meaning and weight; nor would I.

This is what we humans have lost, our place among, not above, I thought, looking over my shoulder at the massive dike behind. I realized that I was not intended by virtue of my biology to see this expansive vista. It's a peculiarly privileged view, looking down on the bobbing iridescent backs of glossy ibis among the thick wetland plantings; the shine of the great lake a mile east of me; and the unbearably vulnerable roosting of a thousand or two swallow-tailed kites in their coming season, just to the south. Living atop our enormous constructs, we have come to believe we deserve to stand apart and above. I imagined sliding the enormity of this dike back into the beds of the canals, staunching the tannic bleeding of the lake and the land to the sea, reshaping the watery balance of the place. I imagined removing the grid of fence, road, dike, canal. I contemplated restoration.

Vultures, a mix of black and turkey, assembled behind and above me as I squatted at the lip of the canal. Did they think I was dying? I said to them: *I am not*. I found myself half-laughing, half-choking back sobs, my human frustration mixed with an inexplicable modicum of joy. A Florida duck arrowed past me, echoing my foolish quacking with its own natural voice.

As I stood and turned, ready to climb the unnatural dike's slope and head home, I knew that if a kite chanced to soar close, I would stir with electric connection, as I always have. But when kites are not nearby, I realized, I could no longer pursue them nor pry their secrets from the scientists. Not chase after, but seek within. This means I must dive for spirit, the invisible river of being that connects us all at one time, all the time. Accept that I cannot always be physically present with the things I love, that there are other places they have to be that I cannot go, not without resources I don't have and the planet can't afford. The kites must power to Brazil every August and will be dispersed over our remotest floodplain forests much of the time they are here. So my life will continue to settle out with less of kites than I wanted when I was seeking them, even though they will always be one of the primary signals that orient me to season and place.

I think back to the teachings of my origin moment, wondering at how the circumstances of my birth have shunted me along this life path, directed me toward a passion for nature, birds, stillness, soft air, isolation, but with the human city still in sight. I see how I play out my people's ancient scarcities, taking more than I need. And I also see in myself pure, instinctual life, greedy only as a child is at the breast in the part-lit dawn, with no more excess or taking. This is a greed that we can safely adapt, I think, the desire for another day with the shape of mountains or swallow-tailed kites in our eyes, the hunger to track the monthly moons, from the apostrophe of the new, to the belly-round full, through the waning. The longing for the weight of the body of mate and child. Greedy for each day of life on this planet: we can know no other.

I understand that inside me, in each of us, is an intact thread of living that extends back through aeons of human birthings and thrustings into life to a time when the hurts we installed on one another and the planet were more animal, before hoarding or malice. I reach for that thread—so like palm fiber—and hold tight.

Afterword

So much more is known about the migratory journeys and habitat requirements of swallow-tailed kites now than when I first began to write about them in 1994. Dr. Ken Meyer of the Avian Research and Conservation Institute is still at the forefront of the science of swallow-tails, but now he's got colleagues in nearly every southeastern state and in South America tracking the elusive birds. You can "watch" the migrations of several of the birds Meyer and others have fitted with satellite transmitters at http://www.adoptabird.org/kitesite/.

If you sign on to the computer list-serve for Florida birds (http://bkpass.tripod.com/FLBIRDS-SUB.htm), you will be alerted to the arrival of the very first kites to make landfall each February. The experienced birders who use this tool are a restrained lot; generally, you see only one or two announcements of a "first of season" for a species on the daily e-mail reports. Apparently it is "old hat" if you report, say, the first great crested flycatcher you hear in your yard when someone else within a couple of hundred miles has already posted that news. Not so with swallow-tails. Such is the excitement they generate that you can practically watch them filter back into their breeding range come spring, county by county. If you are new to kites and wonder where to go to see them, check out this wildlife-viewing Web site, and you'll maximize your chances: http://myfwc.com/viewing/species/swtkite.htm.

Notes

All data concerning swallow-tailed kites in this book were derived from interviews with and scientific papers and reports written by Dr. Kenneth Meyer.

Origin Moment

Page 1, Florida writer Bill Belleville must be credited for the phrase "living origami" to describe the soaring of swallow-tailed kites.

Page 3, For a description of Dagara beliefs about life purpose, see Sobonfu Some, *The Spirit of Intimacy: Ancient African Teachings in the Ways of Relationships* (New York: William Morrow, 1999), 56.

Page 8, Thomas Berry describes the terminal phase of the Cenozoic era we have entered in *The Great Work: Our Way into the Future* (New York: Bell Tower, 1999), 4.

Looking for Love

Page 17, See William Kittredge's *Taking Care: Thoughts about Storytelling and Belief* (Minneapolis: Milkweed Editions, 1999), 20, in which he writes of the need for new stories about the land to foster compassion and caretaking.

Page 23, Source for these data is Reed F. Noss and Robert L. Peters, *Endangered Ecosystems: A Status Report on America's Vanishing Habitat and Wildlife* (Washington, D.C.: Defenders of Wildlife, 1995).

Page 24, Information about this particular deer kill due to flooding in the Everglades Conservation Areas is courtesy of Mike Brooks, Florida Fish and Wildlife Conservation Commission. South Florida's water management system was designed to protect and to serve about two million people; the population in the region has now swelled to above seven million residents and continues to grow faster than populations in Haiti, Mexico, or Bangladesh. Information about human incursions into the greater Everglades ecosystem is widely available; one source is the Friends of the Everglades Web site (www.everglades.org). Especially worthwhile to read is the 2002 *Washington Post* series by Michael Grunwald that is linked to this site.

Unremembered Wings

Page 73, From the poem entitled "Poetry" in *Pablo Neruda: Selected Poems*, ed. Nathaniel Tarn, trans. Anthony Kerrigan (Boston: Houghton Mifflin, 1970), 457.

Page 73, Quote taken from Adrienne Rich's *What Is Found There: Notebooks on Poetry and Politics* (New York: W. W. Norton, 1986), 218.

Lake Okeechobee

Page 83, Linda Hogan's nonfiction and poetry investigates native and non-native ways of thinking and knowing; this quote comes from *Dwellings: A Spiritual History of the Living World* (New York: W. W. Norton, 1995), 83.

Like Shooting at the Moon

Page 89, This description is found in *Frank M. Chapman in Florida: His Journals and Letters*, comp. and ed. Elizabeth S. Austin (Gainesville: University of Florida Press, 1967).

Page 89, For a description of the acquisition and identification of wild birds by some early ornithologists, including Albert Franklyn Ganier, see Eric G. Bolen and Dan Flores, *The Mississippi Kite* (Austin: University of Texas Press, 1993), 88.

Pages 89–90, At the time of Roger Tory Peterson's death, an obituary written by Brigitte Greenberg for the Associated Press appeared in the *Tallahassee Democrat* on July 30, 1996, and includes this quote.

Page 90, This description of the swallow-tailed kite's plight was taken from Thomas D. Burleigh, *Georgia Birds* (Norman: University of Oklahoma Press, 1958), 173.

Death of Birth

Page 104, This information about extinction rates was taken from Edward O. Wilson, *The Diversity of Life* (New York: W. W. Norton, 1999), 29.

Page 104, This quote was taken from a talk given by the poet Linda Hogan at the Key West Writers' Workshop on January 13, 1996.

A Great Big Sucking Sound

Page 105, Information taken from J. Cox, R. Kautz, M. MacLaughlin, and T. Gilbert, *Closing the Gaps in Florida's Wildlife Habitat Conservation System* (Tallahassee: Florida Game and Fresh Water Fish Commission, 1994).

Page 107, Statistics from interview with Florida Game and Fresh Water Fish Commission biologist Kimberly Dryden, August 8, 1995.

Page 108, Quote taken from Adrienne Rich, *What is Found There: Notebooks on Poetry and Politics* (New York: W. W. Norton, 1986), 121.

Page 110, Adrienne Rich, *On Lies, Secrets, and Silence: Selected Prose* (New York: W. W. Norton, 1979), 11.

Page 112, In a three-day Earth Kinship workshop at the University of North Florida in Jacksonville, Florida, Sister Miriam MacGillis (February 2000) offered this and many other images of the human presence in North America. To learn more about her writings and work, go to the Genesis Farm Web site (www.genesisfarm.org).

Page 113, Quote from Barbara Kingsolver in *Small Wonder* (New York: HarperCollins, 2002), 71.

Page 115, Statistics from interview with Florida Game and Fresh Water Fish Commission biologist Kimberly Dryden, August 8, 1995.

The Way We Love a Journey

Page 123, In *The Nature of Generosity* (New York: Alfred A. Knopf, 2000), William Kittredge explores the underpinnings of American, particularly Western, culture.

Fisheating Creek

Page 129, The Fort Center site is now managed by the Florida Fish and Wildlife Conservation Commission and is part of the Fisheating Creek Wildlife Management Area.

Page 130, To learn more about the archaeology of this area, read *Fort Center: An Archaeological Site in the Lake Okeechobee Basin*, ed. William H. Sears, with contributions by Elsie O'R. Sears and Karl T. Steinen (Gainesville: University Press of Florida, 1994).

Page 131, For more about Iban beliefs and practices, see James G. Cowan's *Messengers of the Gods* (New York: Bell Tower, 1993), 75–138.

Page 136, Quote by Terry Tempest Williams in *Leap* (New York: Pantheon, 2000), 118.

Page 138, Malidoma Some, *The Healing Wisdom of Africa: Finding Life Purpose through Nature, Ritual, and Community* (New York: Jeremy P. Tarcher/Putnam, 1998).

Page 139, From the poem "A Great Wagon" by Jalaluddin Rumi in *The Essential Rumi*, trans. Coleman Barks with John Moyne, A. J. Arberry, and Reynold Nicholson (New York: HarperCollins, 1995), 35.

Restorying

Page 141, This quote is from a talk by Linda Hogan at the Thoreau III conference held in Missoula, Montana, in May 1995.

Page 147, For a compelling account of a psychological disease of our times, read Bruce Wilshire's *Wild Hunger: The Primal Roots of Modern Addiction* (Lanham: Rowman and Littlefield, 1998), 41.

Page 148, For more about the indigenous peoples of South America and their spiritual connection to swallow-tailed kites, see *Portals of Power: Shamanism in South America*, ed. E. Jean Matteson Langdon and Gerhard Baer (Albuquerque: University of New Mexico Press, 1992).

Call and Response

Page 159, This quote is taken from a speech given by Muriel Rukeyser, which is included in Adrienne Rich's *What is Found There: Notebooks on Poetry and Politics* (New York: W. W. Norton, 1986), 21.

Acknowledgments

I have raised my son, David Canter, alongside this writing; he is the light of my heart. What extraordinary good fortune to be his mother. On a daily basis, Norine Cardea has accompanied and encouraged me into the unconscious territories of kites and humans both. A more steadfast companion doesn't exist. I'm grateful beyond words for the lifelong conversations and deep commitments I share with Janisse Ray. Her tough insights, unwavering courage, and constant love inspire me always.

In the person of Ken Meyer are blended generosity, a brilliant mind, and an unwavering commitment to his science. He and the kites are a true match, deserving of every superlative. He didn't have to take me on, but he did. Thanks, Ken. Brian Millsap, Jim Cox, and Kim Dryden are among the many scientists who hold the front line for wild things. May your lives be blessed. The appearance of Karla Brandt with the stories I craved amazes me still.

This book was born at the Teller Environmental Writing Institute under the tutelage of Annick Smith and Terry Tempest Williams. I honor their wisdom. Sheila Ortiz Taylor is a wonderful writer and teacher; I'm indebted to her for the practice of keeping a commonplace book. She also directed me to Hedgebrook: my writing retreat there was essential to the building of this book. Thank you to the women who hold that vision.

I owe a great deal to the editorial insights of Patricia Foster and Barrie Jean Borich. Deena Metzger and the Pine Mountain women writers gave this book the final nudge it needed. The poetry and graceful presence of Linda Hogan are always a beacon. Time and again I return to the companionship and forward thinking of southern writers of nature and place: Al Burt, Jan DeBlieu, Janisse Ray, Franklin Burroughs, Julie Hauserman, Bill Belleville, John Lane, Betsy Teter, Thomas Rain Crowe, Renee Zenaida, Jeff Klinkenberg, Melissa Walker, Jeff Ripple, and the late Jim Kilgo.

During the years that I explored the territory of swallow-tailed kites, many friends supported my journey. I am always grateful for the longstanding friendship of Ann Morrow and her many gifts, including child care, time together in the wild, and a cardboard replica of this book to hold a place on my shelf until the real thing appeared! Thanks also to Julie Morris and Jono Miller, always contributing a new angle and an enduring friendship. Loretta Armer and the sisters of Womenspirit have been with me since the beginning. Their love and wisdom hold me. Pieces of this story were written in the incredible company of my Tallahassee writers' circle: Velma Frye, Donna Klein, and Noreen Legare. I'm most grateful to them. To our dear companions Crystal and Lumin Wakoa and David and Marley Moynahan, may our times together be long.

My family is the essential underpinning of all that I do. Special love and gratitude to my parents, Charles R. and Janet Isleib; my stepmothers Mary Jane Isleib and Elise Lawton Isleib; Roberta Isleib and John Brady; Doug and Cindy Isleib; Martha Isleib; and all our children, Patrick and Kate Chanton, Zachary and Brian Isleib, Molly and Andrew Brady, Rachel Jakob, Garrett and Erin Canter, Sophie Cardea Alsop, and Kristin and Vanessa Dozier. It's been a wonderful pleasure to share the business of writing with my sister and companion since birth, Roberta Isleib. Elise Smith and her family are also beloved and have accompanied me in person or in their hearts throughout. Ann Morrow and Susan Canter made it possible for me to travel after kites when David was small; thousands of thanks. Before I was done with my search for kites and what they taught me, my marriage with my son's father ended. But I will always be grateful for his partnership in raising our son, and for his support during the years we were together.

Thank you, also, to members of my community who helped me along the way, including the Heart of the Earth Council (especially Barry Fraser, Lucy Ann Walker-Fraser, Mary Beth McBride, and Mike Brezin), Jim Wohlpart, Gretchen Hein, Linda Taylor, Lora Silvanima, Jan Godown, Ellery Akers, Cadence Kidwell, Mary Jane Ryals and the Blackjavadogs Writers, Doug Alderson, Sharon Rauch, Laura Newton, Wilderness Sarchild, Chuck Madansky, and Andrea Blount. For years spent in the woods and on the rivers, I will always be grateful to Raven Burchard, Nina Hatton, Bob Knight, Penny Jaques, Gary Schultz, Bob Simons, and Tim Fendley.

Christa Frangiamore flew into my life just like a kite, seeking this book for the University of Georgia Press. Thank you, Christa, and all the dedicated and talented staff of the Press, for your vision and your support.

And to the kites: what privilege to follow your lives for a time. May you always fly high.

Most important of all are the thanks I owe to my husband, Jeff Chanton, who has supported my writing as completely as he's committed himself to our life together. Our love is woven of many strands, including science and spirit both. There could be no better partner.